PLATONOV

PLATONOV

An abridged version of
an untitled play in four acts
by
ANTON CHEKHOV

Translated by
DMITRI MAKAROFF

with an Introduction by
George Devine

LONDON
METHUEN & CO LTD
36 ESSEX STREET WC2

First published in Great Britain in 1961

Printed in Great Britain
by W. & J. Mackay & Co Ltd
Chatham, Kent
Catalogue No. 2/6500/1

INTRODUCTION

In spite of the literary controversy that seethes around this play, there seems little doubt that it was Chekhov's first dramatic work and I have always held it to be such. There can hardly exist in dramatic literature a more revealing rough sketch of the lines on which a great dramatist was to develop. We know it was written when he was about 21, and supporting most of his family on his humorous writings. We know that his next dramatic efforts were the one act farces, *The Bear*, *The Proposal*, *The Wedding*, *The Anniversary*. I stress this humorous aspect of the young Chekhov's work at this stage of his career because, when the play was produced at the Royal Court in 1960, an extraordinary idea was put about with considerable vehemence that the play was meant to be entirely serious. A study of the text and stage directions will prove this contention to be entirely fallacious. Even in the near tragic last moments after Platonov has been shot, the Doctor shouts for water, presumably for the patient, and is handed a decanter. 'The doctor drinks the water and throws the decanter aside', says Chekhov's stage direction. If this is not *intended* by the dramatist to be funny, in the midst of the tragedy, I'll be confounded.

The trouble with genius is that people like to adopt it, make it their own and then accuse of vandalism anyone who does not comply with *their* adopted conception of this genius. It is palpably clear from reading the text, which has been assiduously compared by my collaborator, John Blatchley, and myself with a literal translation of the original taken from the archives of Chekhov's work, that the play is a young man's work, containing a rather crude mixture of melodrama and farce, together with the beginnings of that extraordinary sensitive observation of human nature that Chekhov was to develop into his own personal style. Later the melodrama and farce were refined into the tragi-comedy we all know so well. Even over these later masterpieces, Chekhov himself quarrelled with Stanislavsky and the Moscow Arts Theatre actors because they performed his plays too seriously. They are called by him 'Comedies'.

It is not easy in performance to control the movement from the serious to the comic, and vice versa. The Russian temperament is more volatile than the English—it swings more quickly from laughter to tears, and back. But this is an issue directors and actors must face. If they do, squarely, the results will prove rewarding.

As for the text, this version can claim some originality in that it contains the first act which most productions of the play have omitted hitherto. Blatchley and I stumbled on this first act by chance a few weeks before we went into rehearsal. It was a revelation and gave the play its frame as a social commentary on the young intellectuals who had failed to take their responsibilities in the changing political climate of Russia. In order to contain this first act, we had to re-examine, together with Dmitri Makaroff, the translator, the whole five acts, which, in their entirety, would have played over four hours, and reduce them to a playable length of three, while attempting to preserve all the essential threads woven in by the dramatist.

We can assure the theatre man that the play is difficult to perform but works wonderfully on the stage. The scholar and student will find it a mine of interest for the characters and themes which are later to be compressed and developed. The only theme which never recurs is that of the Jews—Vengerovitch and his son. They disappear for ever after this play, although Chekhov clearly felt them strongly when writing it.

GEORGE DEVINE

NOTES ON THE PLAY

This work was Chekhov's first play, but was never presented or even published during his lifetime.

The play was first discovered in about 1920, when the Chekhov family papers passed into the Central State Literary Archives, Moscow. The manuscript consists of eleven home-made exercise books, and covers 134 pages. There is no title page, and the manuscript is not dated. On the basis of the handwriting, the play can be regarded as belonging to the early 1880s. The manuscript bears the marks of numerous cuts made by the author. There is no doubt that this is the very same play mentioned by Mikhail Chekhov in his introductory article to the second volume of *Letters of A. P. Chekhov*: 'While he was a student he wrote a long play with the ardent hope of having it presented on the stage of the Maly Theatre, Moscow. He even presented it to the famous actress, M. N. Yermolova, to read'.

The play has been published in Russian three times: in 1923, under the title of *Unpublished Play by A. P. Chekhov*, by the Central State Literary Archives, Moscow, giving Chekhov's full text and including all cuts within brackets; and in the 1933 and 1949 editions of the complete works of Chekhov, these giving the play as cut by Chekhov. In 1933 the title was given as *Bezotsovshchina* (an untranslatable word which could be freely rendered as 'Sons Without Fathers'), and in 1939 the play was simply described as a *Play Without a Title*.

DMITRI MAKAROFF

SOME NOTES ON RUSSIAN NAMES

In the past it has been the practice on the English stage simply to anglicise the pronunciation of Russian names, often with comic, if not grotesque results. With the ever increasing knowledge of the Russian language that is growing in this country, a rather more careful approach to this problem is indicated, and the following remarks may be of some help to directors and actors who happen to have some consideration for Russian-understanding ears.

It is important to remember that the use of the first name and patronymic by Russians (e.g. Nikolai Ivanovich, Nicholas, son of Ivan) is purely formal and does not imply any intimacy beyond ordinary, everyday acquaintance. If the director should feel that the plethora of 'evich' and 'ovna' is too much both for actors and audience, he should not, on any account, change the combination of Christian name and patronymic to the simple use of the Christian name, as this would imply a more intimate relationship than the one indicated by the author. 'Sir', 'Madam' or Mr. or Mrs. with the surname, or, in the last resort, simple omission would be the only proper substitutes.

In actual practice Russians tend to pronounce the two words together as one and to slur over a number of the sounds. The names occurring in this play could, from the point of view of actual pronunciation, be transcribed as follows: Anna Petrovna: annpitróvna; Sergei Pavlovich: sirgyeipálch; Sofya Yegorovna: sofy'góravna; Porfiri Semyonovich: parfiry'simyónch; Kiril Porfiryevich: kirilparfírch; Pavel Petrovich: palpitróich; Marya Yefimovna: mary'fímna; Ivan Ivanovich: vanvánch; Nikolai Ivanovich: niklaivánch; Abram Abramovich: abrambrámch; Isak Abramovich: isakabrámch; Timofei Gordeyevich: timfyeigardyéich; Mikhail Vasilyevich: mihalvasílch; Alexandra Ivanovna: sanvána.

The vowels should have a pure sound, more or less as in Italian; 'y' should have a palatal sound as in 'you'.

D.M.

THE CHARACTERS

ANNA PETROVNA VÓINITSEVA,[1] a general's young widow

SERGEI PAVLOVICH VÓINITSEV, her step-son, a bankrupt

SOFYA YEGOROVNA (SOPHIE), his wife

PORFIRI SEMYONOVICH GLAGÓLYEV
KIRIL PORFIRYEVICH GLAGÓLYEV, his son
GERASIM KUZMICH PÉTRIN (GERÁSYA)
PAVEL PETROVICH SHCHERBÚK (PÁVA, PÁVOCHKA)
MARYA YEFIMOVNA GRÉKOVA, a girl of twenty
} landowners, neighbours of the Voinitsevs

IVAN IVANOVICH TRILÉTSKI, a retired colonel

NIKOLAI IVANOVICH TRILÉTSKI, his son, a young doctor

ABRAM ABRAMOVICH VENGEROVICH, a rich Jewish business man

ISAK ABRAMOVICH VENGERÓVICH, his son, a student[2]

TIMOFEI GORDEYEVICH BUGRÓV, a merchant, agent to Vengerovich

MIKHAIL VASILYEVICH PLATÓNOV (MÍSHA, MICHEL), a village schoolmaster

ALEXANDRA IVANOVNA (SÁSHA), his wife, daughter of Ivan Triletski

ÓSIP, a thirty-year-old peasant, a horse-thief

MARKO, messenger of the Justice of the Peace, a little old man

VASILI
YAKOV
KATYA
} servants of the Voinitsevs

GUESTS, SERVANTS

The action takes place on the Voinitsev estate in one of the southern provinces.

[1]The accents indicate the correct position of the stress. For the pronunciation of other names, see p.8

[2]This part was omitted in the Royal Court Theatre production.

This play was first presented in England at the Royal Court Theatre, London, on 13 October 1960, with the following cast:

ANNA PETROVNA	Rachel Roberts
NIKOLAI TRILÉTSKI	Ronald Barker
SERGEI VÓINITSEV	Graham Crowden
GLAGÓLYEV	Norman Pitt
VENGEROVICH	Nicholas Selby
BUGRÓV	Thomas Hammerton
MIKHAIL PLATÓNOV (MISHA)	Rex Harrison
SÁSHA	Mary Watson
IVAN TRILÉTSKI	Frank Finlay
PÉTRIN	Peter Duguid
MARYA GRÉKOVA	Rosalind Knight
SOFYA (SOPHIE)	Elvi Hale
SHCHERBUK	Jeremy Geidt
VASILI	Morris Perry
ÓSIP	George Murcell
YAKOV	James Bolam
KIRIL	Peter Bowles
KATYA	Susan Engel
DUNYASHA	Susan Westerby
A VILLAGE PRIEST	Murray Gilmore
MARKO	Peter Duguid

The play was directed by George Devine and John Blatchley

Act One

The drawing-room of the Voinitsev house. A french window leading into the garden and two doors leading to other rooms of the house. An assortment of old-fashioned and modern furniture. A grand piano, near it a music stand with violin and music. A harmonium. Pictures (oleographs) in gilt frames.

ANNA PETROVNA *is seated at the grand piano, her head bowed over the keys.* NIKOLAI IVANOVICH TRILETSKI *enters.*

NIKOLAI TRILETSKI (*going up to* ANNA). What is the matter?

ANNA (*raising her head*). Nothing . . . Bored . . .

NIKOLAI TRILETSKI. Give me a cigarette, mon ange. The flesh craves tobacco.

ANNA (*hands him cigarettes*). Take more now and don't come bothering me later. (*They smoke.*) Mon Dieu, quel ennui, Nicolas, quel ennui mortel . . . (TRILETSKI *takes her by the hand.*) Is that to feel my pulse? I'm quite well.

NIKOLAI TRILETSKI. No, it's not your pulse. (*He kisses her hand.*) Chess?

ANNA. Yes, let's . . . (*She looks at the clock.*) Quarter past twelve . . . Our guests must be starving . . .

NIKOLAI TRILETSKI (*setting out the chessboard*). In all probability. I'm ravenous myself.

ANNA. You're always ravenous. Eat, eat, eat! It's terrible! Such a little fellow and such an enormous stomach! (*She sits down to the board.*) Your move . . . You've moved already! You should think first and then move. (*He starts to sing.*) Keep quiet. You're stopping me from thinking.

NIKOLAI TRILETSKI. Why think? Move without thinking, votre excellence. Watch your knight . . . Ye-es . . .

ANNA. What are you gaping at? It's your move. Well, what do you think, is your 'she' coming here today or not?

NIKOLAI TRILETSKI. She promised to come. Gave her word.

ANNA. Then it's time she was here. Is it – forgive a personal question – is it really serious this time? Frankly now, joking apart, does Grekova mean anything to you? I ask you as a friend.

NIKOLAI TRILETSKI. I don't know. I call on her every other day, chat, make a nuisance of myself, run up her mother's coffee bills and . . . that's all. Your move. She holds me by this button here and picks the fluff off my lapel. I'm always covered in fluff, as you know.

ANNA. Well, go on!

NIKOLAI TRILETSKI. Well, that's all. Is it boredom or love that draws me to her, or something else . . . I can't say. I do know that after dinner I get a terrible longing for her . . .

ANNA. Then it's love!

NIKOLAI TRILETSKI (*shrugs*). It may very well be. What do you think, do I love her or not? Your move.

ANNA. I like her. What's she up to nowadays?

NIKOLAI TRILETSKI. She reads . . .

ANNA. And studies chemistry? (*She laughs.*) I like her with her little pointed nose. She might make a fine scientist . . . Look, Nicholas, ask her to come and see me a little more often. Let me get to know her. I'm not going to play the match-maker, it's just that . . . Are you listening to me?

NIKOLAI TRILETSKI. Look! I'm all ears!

ANNA. I know you. You do everything without thinking, and you'll go and marry without thinking. Yes . . . It's no use trusting that silly head of yours. (*She knocks on the table.*) That's what your head's made of! (*She starts to whistle.*)

NIKOLAI TRILETSKI. Hark at her whistling like a peasant! Fantastic woman! (*Pause.*) She won't come to visit you.

ANNA. Why not?

NIKOLAI TRILETSKI. Because you have Platonov gadding about here. She can't abide him with all his tricks . . . The fellow's got it into his head that she's a fool, and for some reason or other he considers it his duty to make a nuisance of himself to all foolish women. Your move.

ANNA. We won't allow him to take any liberties. Tell her not to worry. And why is Platonov so long coming? (*She looks at the clock.*) It's bad manners. We haven't seen each other for six months.

Enter PORFIRI GLAGOLYEV *and* VOINITSEV.

PORFIRI GLAGOLYEV (*entering*). Yes, my dear Sergei Pavlovich. In our day we believed in woman, loved her, worshipped her . . . (*They sit.*)

ANNA. But why cheat?

NIKOLAI TRILETSKI. Who's cheating?

ANNA. And who put this pawn here?

NIKOLAI TRILETSKI. But you put it there yourself!

ANNA. Oh yes . . . Pardon! (*In French.*)

NIKOLAI TRILETSKI (*mimicking her sarcastically*). Pardon!

PORFIRI GLAGOLYEV. And friendship wasn't a superficial thing. We were expected to go through fire for a friend.

VOINITSEV (*yawning*). A fine time it must have been!

NIKOLAI TRILETSKI. And in these terrible days of ours we keep firemen to go through fire for friends.

ANNA. That's silly, Nicholas. (*There is a pause.*)

PORFIRI GLAGOLYEV. Last winter in Moscow at the opera I saw a young man weep because he was so moved by the music . . . Would you say that that's a good thing?

VOINITSEV. A very good thing, I should have thought.

PORFIRI GLAGOLYEV. And I too think it's a very good thing. But then why, tell me please, why did all the ladies and their escorts sitting near by snigger at him? What were they laughing at? In our day people weren't ashamed of healthy tears nor did they laugh at them. You're yawning, Sergei Pavlovich, I'm boring you.

VOINITSEV. No, but what does all this add up to, Porfiri Semyonovich?

PORFIRI GLAGOLYEV. Well . . . It all adds up to the fact that in our day we . . .

ANNA. I can't go on! He reeks so of his insufferable scent, I feel quite ill! Anyway I want to listen to Porfiri Semyonovich. I've had enough chess. I'm tired of it. (*She rises.*)

NIKOLAI TRILETSKI. When I'm losing she sits there rooted to the spot, but now that she's losing it's the scent that's to blame *and* she takes a fancy to listening to Porfiri Semyonovich! (*To* GLAGOLYEV.) And who asked you to talk? You're only spoiling the game! (*To* ANNA.) Sit down and play on, if you please, otherwise I'll take it you've lost!

ANNA. Take it as you will. (*She sits opposite* PORFIRI GLAGOLYEV.)

Enter ABRAM VENGEROVICH.

ABRAM VENGEROVICH (*entering*). It's hot! This heat reminds a Yid like me of Palestine. (*He sits at the piano and runs his fingers over the keys.*)

NIKOLAI TRILETSKI (*rising*). And so we'll note it down, my dear woman! (*In his notebook.*) Debit the general's lady with three roubles. Total owing with previous losses – ten. Aha! And when shall I be having the honour of receiving this sum from you?

ANNA. Sergei, give this church beggar ten roubles.

VOINITSEV. Ten? (*Taking out his wallet.*) Well, let's change the conversation, Porfiri Semyonovich . . .

NIKOLAI TRILETSKI. Merci. (*He slaps* ABRAM VENGEROVICH *on the shoulder.*) That's the way to live. You take on a defenceless woman at chess, and without the least compunction clean her out of ten shekels! How's that, eh? Praiseworthy?

ABRAM VENGEROVICH. Very praiseworthy! I can see, doctor, that you're a high-class Jerusalem aristocrat!

ANNA. Stop it, Triletski! (*To* GLAGOLYEV.) So it seems that you're very fond of women, Porfiri Semyonovich!

PORFIRI GLAGOLYEV. Yes, Anna Petrovna, I am. I respect and adore them . . .

ANNA. Yes, but do they deserve your adoration?

NIKOLAI TRILETSKI *picks up the violin and scrapes with the bow.*

PORFIRI GLAGOLYEV. They do. Knowing you alone is enough to convince me . . .

VOINITSEV. He's a romantic!

PORFIRI GLAGOLYEV. Perhaps. Romanticism is by no means a bad thing. You've banished romanticism. No doubt you've done well, but I fear that together with it you've banished something else.

ANNA. No polemics, please, my friend! I'm no good at arguing. Whether we've banished it or not, we have, in any case, thank God, grown wiser. We *have* grown wiser, haven't we, Porfiri Semyonovich? And that's the main thing . . . (*She laughs.*) As long as we have people getting wiser, the rest will come of itself . . . Oh! Do stop scraping at that violin, Nikolai Ivanovich! Put it down!

NIKOLAI TRILETSKI (*hanging up the violin*). A fine instrument!

PORFIRI GLAGOLYEV. Platonov once put it very well. Nowadays, he said, our attitude to women is much more intelligent, and when one's attitude to women is much more intelligent, it simply means that one drags them and oneself into the mire . . .

NIKOLAI TRILETSKI (*laughing loudly*). It must have been his birthday!

ANNA. He said that? (*She laughs.*) Yes, he likes to come out with these pronouncements. Tell me, in your opinion, what kind of a man is this Platonov? Is he a hero, or not a hero?

PORFIRI GLAGOLYEV. How can I put it? Platonov, I think, embodies all the indeterminacy of our society today. He's the hero of the very best modern novel, not yet written, alas! (*He laughs.*) Our novelists here in Russia have . . . reached a dead end, they don't know what to catch hold of! The novels couldn't be worse! No wonder! Everything is so utterly vague and incomprehensible. It's all so very involved. Now in my opinion it's this vagueness that finds such perfect expression in our learned Platonov. Is he well?

ANNA. They say he is. (*A pause.*) A nice man.

PORFIRI GLAGOLYEV. Yes, I called on him several times this winter and I shall never forget those hours I was fortunate enough to spend with him.

ANNA (*looking at her watch*). It's time he was here. Sergei, did you send for him?

VOINITSEV. Twice.

ANNA. Triletski, run and send Yakov to fetch him!

NIKOLAI TRILETSKI (*stretching himself*). Shall I tell them to serve lunch?

ANNA. I'll tell them myself.

BUGROV *enters.*

NIKOLAI TRILETSKI (*bumping into* BUGROV *at the door*). Here he comes, the grocery man, puffing like a steam engine! (*He slaps him on the stomach and goes out.*)

BUGROV. Oof! Terrible, the heat! There's rain on the way, to be sure!

VOINITSEV. Have you come from the garden? Is Sophie there?

BUGROV. What Sophie?

VOINITSEV. My wife, Sofya Yegorovna.

Exit ABRAM VENGEROVICH *into the garden.* PLATONOV *and* SASHA (*the latter in Russian costume*) *enter.*

PLATONOV (*at the door, to* SASHA). Please, after you, young woman! (*He enters after* SASHA.) Well, here we are at last! How do you do, Your Excellency! (*He comes up to* ANNA, *kisses one hand and then the other.*)

ANNA. Cruel, ill-mannered fellow . . . To have made me wait so long! Dearest Alexandra Ivanovna . . . (*She kisses* SASHA.)

PLATONOV. At long last, thank the Lord! Six months we haven't seen parquet floors, or high ceilings, or arm-chairs, or even people. We've slept through the whole winter like bears in a den and . . . Sergei Pavlovich! (*He embraces* VOINITSEV.)

VOINITSEV. He's put on weight! What the devil! Alexandra Ivanovna, you've been putting on weight too! (*He shakes hands with her.*) Are you well? *And* you're looking prettier!

PLATONOV (*shakes* PORFIRI GLAGOLYEV'S *hand*). Porfiri Semyonovich! So very happy to see you!

ANNA. And how are you, Alexandra Ivanovna? But do sit down, please, everyone! Tell us all the news . . . Let's sit! (*They all sit. To* PLATONOV.) How has it been, Mikhail Vasilyevich?

PLATONOV. As nasty as ever. Slept through the whole winter, didn't see the sky once in six months. Drank, ate, slept . . . ugh! How one yearned for you! But now, just to *see* you, Anna Petrovna, after all that wearisome emptiness – why, it's an unforgivable luxury!

ANNA. Take a cigarette for that! (*She gives him a cigarette.*)

PLATONOV. Merci. (*They smoke.*)

SASHA. You arrived yesterday evening?

ANNA. At nine o'clock. Why didn't you come? . . .

PLATONOV. At eleven we saw your lights were on, but we thought you'd be tired . . .

ANNA. Tired! Why, we sat up talking till two.

SASHA *whispers in* PLATONOV'S *ear.*

PLATONOV. Hell! (*He hits himself on the forehead.*) What a memory! (*To* SASHA.) Why didn't you remind me before? Sergei Pavlovich!

VOINITSEV. What?

PLATONOV. nd h e doesn't say a word! Goes and gets married and doesn't say a word! (*He rises.*) I forget and they none of them say a word!

SASHA. Congratulations, Sergei Pavlovich! I wish you . . . everything . . .

PLATONOV. My dear fellow, permit me . . . (*He bows.*) A miracle, Sergei Pavlovich! So soon, so quick! Whoever could have expected such heresy of you?

VOINITSEV. How's that, eh? So soon, so quick! (*He laughs.*) I didn't expect such heresy of me myself! The deal was done in the twinkling of an eye. Fell in love . . . Married! . . .

PLATONOV. And have you found a job yet?

VOINITSEV. I've been offered a place in a prep school, but they don't pay much and I don't . . .

ANNA (*changing the subject*). Oh, it's too hot! . . . But why have you been so long coming, Alexandra Ivanovna?

SASHA. I went to Father Constantine to order a requiem for Misha's poor father. Today would have been his name day. It wouldn't have been right not to have said a prayer for him . . .

Pause.

PORFIRI GLAGOLYEV. How long is it since your father died, Mikhail Vasilyevich?

PLATONOV. Some three or four years . . .

SASHA. Three years and eight months.

PORFIRI GLAGOLYEV. Heavens, how time flies! It seems only the other day I saw him for the last time! (*He sighs.*)

Yes, we were both serving as jurymen . . . (*He sighs.*) They were trying some little drunkard of a surveyor for extortion and (*laughing*) we acquitted him . . . Your father insisted on it! He was so angry! 'I refuse to pass judgement on him,' he cried, 'until you all swear on oath that you do not take bribes!' And the late General Voinitsev, your husband, was there with us too, Anna Petrovna. Another man with a mind of his own!

ANNA. *He* would never have acquitted him!

PORFIRI GLAGOLYEV. Indeed no, he pressed for a conviction. I remember them both, red in the face, spluttering with fury. (*He laughs.*) Your father challenged the general to a duel; the general had called him a blackguard! (*He chuckles.*) We got them drunk afterwards and they made it up. It's the easiest thing to make the peace between Russians. He was a kind fellow, your father. He had a kind heart.

PLATONOV. Not kind . . . just careless.

PORFIRI GLAGOLYEV. We were great friends.

PLATONOV. Well, that's something I can't boast of. I didn't respect him; he considered me a shallow, frivolous fellow and . . . we were both right. For the last three years of his life we were enemies. I can't forgive him for having died peacefully. He died as honest men should die. To be a villain and at the same time not to want to admit it: that's the terrible peculiarity of the Russian scoundrel!

PORFIRI GLAGOLYEV. De mortuis aut bene aut nihil, Mikhail Vasilyevich!

Enter IVAN TRILETSKI.

IVAN TRILETSKI. So-so-so! My son-in-law and daughter! Luminaries from the constellation of Colonel Triletski! How are you, my darlings? A salute to you from a Krupp gun! Lord, how hot it is! Míshenka, my poppet . . .

PLATONOV (*rising*). Hello, colonel! (*He embraces him.*) Are you well?

IVAN TRILETSKI. I'm always well. The Lord is patient and withholds his punishments. Sáshenka! (*He kisses her on the head.*)

ANNA. Darling Ivan Ivanovich! We're going to go shooting quail with him on St. Peter's Day.

IVAN TRILETSKI. Ho-ho! And we'll go a-campaigning against the snipe, Anna Petrovna . . . and then a polar expedition to Devil's Marsh!

ANNA. We'll try out that new English double-barrelled gun of yours . . .

IVAN TRILETSKI. We'll try it out, divine Artemis! (*Kissing her hand.*) Ha, ha! Smite me down, Lord, but I like such women! You just take a sniff at her shoulder and it's gunpowder, Hannibals and Hamilcars she smells of! Yes, and we'll take Sashka with us – we'll take everyone! We'll show them what martial blood means, divine Artemis! Alexandra the Great of Macedon!

PLATONOV. You've had a nip already, colonel?

IVAN TRILETSKI. Of course . . . Sans doute . . .

PLATONOV. So that's why you've set up such a cackling!

IVAN TRILETSKI. Well, I got here at eight. Everyone was still in bed; suddenly I looked and there she was, Artemis, coming out of the house laughing, so we polished off a bottle of Madeira between us. Her Excellency had three glasses – I had the rest!

ANNA. That's right! Now go and tell everyone!

Enter NIKOLAI TRILETSKI, *running.*

PLATONOV. A-a-a! Her Excellency's good-for-nothing medical officer! Argentum nitricum! Aquae destilate! It's good to see you dear fellow! Healthy, radiant, scintillating and fragrant!

NIKOLAI TRILETSKI (*kissing* SASHA'S *head*). What the hell have you been feeding him? Look at him! (*Pointing to* PLATONOV.)

SASHA. Pooh! How you smell of scent!

PLATONOV. What an excellent haircut! Must have cost a whole rouble!

NIKOLAI TRILETSKI. It's not a barber's handiwork. I have ladies to do the job! And it's not for cutting my hair that I give them roubles! . . . I . . .

PLATONOV. More humour! No! No! No! Don't bother! Spare us, do!

PETRIN *enters with a newspaper and sits down.* ABRAM VENGEROVICH *enters and sits in a corner.*

NIKOLAI TRILETSKI (*sitting next to* BUGROV). The temperament is hot today, isn't it, Timofei Gordeyevich?

BUGROV. That's so. It's like a steam bath on the very top shelf. A temperament of thirty degrees or so, I'd say.

NIKOLAI TRILETSKI. Now what could this mean? Why should it be so hot? Timofei Gordeyevich?

BUGROV. Well I'd say, why it's so hot's because you and I'd start laughing if it was cold right now in the month of June.

There is laughter.

NIKOLAI TRILETSKI. So that's it. Now I understand. What would you say is better for the grass, Timofei Gordeyevich, climate or atmosphere?

BUGROV. They're both very good, Nikolai Ivanovich, only for the crops a little rain'd be much better. What use's climate if there's no rain? Not worth a brass farthing without rain.

NIKOLAI TRILETSKI. Quod erat demonstrandum! You're a clever man, Timofei Gordeyevich, wisdom itself drops from your lips! Well, and of what opinion would you be, Mister Grocery Man, regarding such an astronomical conjuring trick as Anna Petrovna giving us something to eat? Eh?

ANNA. Oh, I'm so *sick* of him! His impertinence is positively disgraceful! All right, just you wait there, you horrid man! *I'll* give you something to eat! (*She goes out.*)

NIKOLAI TRILETSKI. High time too!

VOINITSEV (*to* PLATONOV). Michel, you haven't met my wife yet. I must introduce you. (*Rising.*) I'll go and look for her.

PLATONOV. By the way, Sergei Pavlovich, don't introduce me to your wife. I'd like to see if she recognises me. I used to know her once . . .

VOINITSEV. You knew her? You knew Sonya?

PLATONOV. I was still a student then. Don't introduce me, please, and don't say a word to her about me . . .

VOINITSEV. The man knows absolutely everyone. Whenever does he find the time? (*He goes out into the garden.*)

NIKOLAI TRILETSKI. Have you read that excellent article of mine in the 'Russian Courier', gentlemen? Have you? Have you read it, Abram Abramovich?

ABRAM VENGEROVICH. I have.

NIKOLAI TRILETSKI. First rate, wasn't it? And what about you? What a cannibal it made you out to be, eh, Abram Abramovich? Why, it's going to scare the whole of Europe out of its wits, what I've said about you!

PETRIN. So that's who it was about! So that's who 'V' is! Well then, who is 'B'?

BUGROV (*laughing*). That's me! (*He mops his brow.*)

ABRAM VENGEROVICH. Well, and very praiseworthy it is too! Only it wasn't you, doctor, that wrote it. It was Porfiri Semyonovich here.

PORFIRI GLAGOLYEV. How did you know?

ABRAM VENGEROVICH. I just know.

PORFIRI GLAGOLYEV. Strange . . . Yes I wrote it all right, but how did you find out?

ABRAM VENGEROVICH. You can find out anything if you set your mind to it. You sent it off by registered mail. Well, the post office clerk has a good memory, that's all! Don't be afraid, I shan't seek revenge.

PORFIRI GLAGOLYEV. I'm not afraid . . . I just find it rather strange . . .

Enter MARYA GREKOVA.

NIKOLAI TRILETSKI (*jumping up*). Marya Yefimovna! But how very nice! But what a surprise!

GREKOVA (*giving him her hand*). How do you do, Nikolai Ivanovich! (*She nods to all those present in the room.*) How do you do!

NIKOLAI TRILETSKI (*taking off her talma*). Are you well? (*He kisses her hand.*)

GREKOVA (*obviously embarrassed and sitting on the first chair to hand*). Is Anna Petrovna at home?

NIKOLAI TRILETSKI. She is. (*He sits beside her.*)

PORFIRI GLAGOLYEV. How do you do, Marya Yefimovna!

IVAN TRILETSKI. Is it Marya Yefimovna? I hardly recognized you! (*He comes up and kisses her hand.*) Very happy to see you . . . indeed . . .

GREKOVA. How do you do, Ivan Ivanovich! (*She coughs.*) Please dont kiss my hand . . . It embarrasses me . . . I don't like it . . .

PLATONOV (*approaching her*). My humble respects! (*He tries to kiss her hand.*) How are you? Well, give me your hand, then!

GREKOVA (*pulling her hand back brusquely*). There's no need . . .

PLATONOV. Why? Am I unworthy?

GREKOVA. I don't know whether you're worthy or not, but . . . after all, it's not sincere, is it?

PLATONOV. Not sincere? But how do you know?

GREKOVA. You wouldn't have wanted to kiss my hand if I hadn't said that I don't care for it . . . But then you always like doing what I dislike.

PLATONOV. Swift conclusion!

NIKOLAI TRILETSKI (*to* PLATONOV). Go away!

PLATONOV. One moment. How is your ether of bed-bugs, Marya Yefimovna?

GREKOVA. What ether?

PLATONOV. I heard that you were distilling an ether from bed-bugs. You want to enrich science. A fine thing . . .

GREKOVA (*rising*). Why do you say all that to me?

PLATONOV. I want to talk to you. Now, don't get angry! Enfin, when are you going to stop losing your temper with me?

GREKOVA. I've noticed that you never feel quite yourself when you see me. I don't know what I do to bother you, but . . . I do you the pleasure of avoiding you as much as possible. If Nikolai Ivanovich hadn't given me his word of honour that you wouldn't be here, I certainly shouldn't have come. (*To* NIKOLAI TRILETSKI.) You should be ashamed to lie! (*She goes quickly to the door where she meets* ANNA *entering*.)

NIKOLAI TRILETSKI (*to* PLATONOV). Fool! Just once more and . . . we're enemies!

PLATONOV. And what have you to do with all this?

PORFIRI GLAGOLYEV. You're cruel, Mikhail Vasilyevich!

ANNA. Marya Yefimovna! How happy I am! (*They shake hands.*) So happy! You come to see me so rarely! Shall we sit down? (*They sit down.*)

NIKOLAI TRILETSKI. Suppose I love her, what then?

PLATONOV. Go on, love her . . . Do us the favour!

ANNA. And how are you, my dear?

GREKOVA. Quite well, thank you.

ANNA. You're worn out. (*Looking up into her face.*) No wonder; twenty versts when you're not used to it . . .

GREKOVA. No . . . (*She begins to weep, covering her eyes with her handkerchief.*) No . . .

ANNA. What's the matter with you, Marya Yefimovna?

There is a pause.

GREKOVA. No . . .

NIKOLAI TRILETSKI *begins to pace up and down.*

PORFIRI GLAGOLYEV (*to* PLATONOV). You must apologise, Mikhail Vasilyevich! You were cruel!

PLATONOV. Why?

SASHA (*coming up to* PLATONOV). Say you're sorry or I leave . . .

ANNA. I often cry myself after long journeys . . . Nerves . . .

PORFIRI GLAGOLYEV. Enfin! I demand it! It's ill-mannered! I never expected it of you!

SASHA. Apologise, I tell you! You're shameless!

ANNA. I understand. (*She looks at* PLATONOV.) Forgive me, Marya Yefimovna. I forgot to have a talk with this . . . this . . . It's my fault . . .

PLATONOV (*coming up to her*). Marya Yefimovna!

GREKOVA (*raising her head*). What do you want?

PLATONOV. I apologise. In front of all these people I ask your forgiveness. Give me your hand then. On my honour, this is sincere. (*Taking her hand.*) Let's make peace. No more whimpering. Peace? (*He kisses her hand.*)

GREKOVA. Peace. (*She buries her face in her handkerchief and runs out followed by* NIKOLAI TRILETSKI.)

ANNA. To take such a liberty! You!

PLATONOV. Pah! (*He sits down on a divan.*) I was a fool to have spoken to her . . .

Enter VOINITSEV *and* SOFYA YEGOROVNA *followed by* ISAK VENGEROVICH.

VOINITSEV (*running in*). She's coming! She's coming! (*He sings.*) She's coming!

ISAK VENGEROVICH *stands by the door, arms folded.*

ANNA. At last Sophie has decided to take shelter from this insufferable heat! Come, my dear . . .

PLATONOV (*aside*). Sonya! God in heaven, how she's changed!

SOFYA (*sits on the divan two feet away from* PLATONOV). I'm in raptures with our garden, Sergei! I simply didn't notice the heat.

PORFIRI GLAGOLYEV (*sitting down beside* SOFYA). Sergei Pavlovich, my dear friend Sofya Yegorovna has given me her word that you're all coming to see me on Thursday next.

VOINITSEV. We shall most certainly keep her word!

NIKOLAI TRILETSKI (*entering*). Oh, women, women! So said Shakespeare and he was wrong. He should have said: Ooo you, women, women!

There is a pause.

ANNA. Silence . . . Somewhere a fool's been born. (*All laugh.*)

SOFYA (*speaking in a soft voice to* PORFIRI GLAGOLYEV *and nodding at* PLATONOV). Who is this sitting next to me?

PORFIRI GLAGOLYEV (*laughing*). It's the local schoolmaster . . . Don't know the name . . .

BUGROV (*to* NIKOLAI TRILETSKI). And is it any sickness at, all you can cure, Nikolai Ivanovich, or not?

NIKOLAI TRILETSKI. Any complaint at all.

BUGROV. And what if a mad dog bit me, could you cure that too?

NIKOLAI TRILETSKI. Has a mad dog bitten you? (*He moves away from him. There is general laughter.*)

SOFYA. And what road should we take to reach you, Porfiri Semyonovich?

PORFIRI GLAGOLYEV. Drive straight to the old Platonov estate. It's only two versts from there.

SOFYA. Platonov! I used to know Platonov. Sergei, where is that man Platonov now?

VOINITSEV. I think I know. You don't happen to remember his name, do you? (*He laughs.*)

PLATONOV. I used to know him once, too. I think he's called Mikhail Vasilyevich. (*Everyone laughs.*)

SOFYA. Yes, yes . . . Mikhail Vasilyevich. When I knew him he was still a student, almost a boy . . . You're all laughing . . . I really can't see anything witty in what I'm saying . . .

ANNA (*laughing loudly and pointing at* PLATONOV). Recognise him, do, or he'll burst with impatience!

PLATONOV *rises.*

SOFYA (*rises and looks at him*). Yes . . . It is . . . Why don't you say anything, Mikhail Vasilyevich? Is it really you?

PLATONOV. Don't you recognise me, Sofya Yegorovna? Small wonder! It's four and a half years, nearly five, and the rats have been at my face!

SOFYA (*giving him her hand*). How you've changed!

VOINITSEV (*leading* SASHA *to* SOFYA). And this is his wife, Alexandra Ivanovna, sister of that wittiest of men, Nikolai Ivanovich!

SOFYA (*shaking hands*). How do you do! (*She sits.*) And so you're married now, too! Five years, of course . . .

ANNA. Bravo, Platonov! He never goes anywhere, yet he knows everyone! I commend him to you, Sofya, he's our friend!

SOFYA. And how are you? What are you doing now?

PLATONOV. Fate has played a trick with me that I could never have foreseen in those days when you saw in me a second Byron and I saw in myself the future minister of some very extra special affairs *and* Christopher Columbus. I'm a schoolmaster, Sofya Yegorovna, just that.

SOFYA. You!

PLATONOV. Yes, me . . . (*There is a pause.*) I suppose it is rather strange . . .

SOFYA. It's incredible! But why . . . why not something? . . .

PLATONOV. I'd need more than one sentence to answer that question, Sofya Yegorovna . . . (*There is a pause.*)

SOFYA. At least you graduated from university?

PLATONOV. No, I threw it up . . .

SOFYA. Hm . . . Still, that doesn't stop you from being a man, does it?

PLATONOV. I'm sorry . . . I don't understand you.

SOFYA. I didn't express myself clearly enough. It doesn't stop you from being a man . . . a working man . . . I mean, engaged in some activity or other . . . well, for instance, freedom, the emancipation of women . . . It doesn't stop you from working for some ideal? . . .

NIKOLAI TRILETSKI (*aside*). What stuff!

PLATONOV (*aside*). So that's it? Hm . . . (*To her.*) Well, how shall I put it? I suppose it doesn't really stop me in any way, but why on earth should it? (*He laughs.*)

Enter SHCHERBUK.

SHCHERBUK (*at the door*). Don't give the horses any oats! They drove badly!

ANNA. Hurrah! My cavalier's here!

ALL. Pavel Petrovich!

SHCHERBUK (*silently he kisses* ANNA'S *and* SASHA'S *hands, silently bows to all the gentlemen in turn, then makes a general bow to the whole company*). My friends, tell me, an unworthy creature, where is that personage whom my soul aspires to behold? I suspect, indeed I think, that this person is she! (*He indicates* SOFYA.) Anna Petrovna, permit me to ask you to commend me to her that she may know what man I am!

ANNA (*taking him by the arm, and leading him to* SOFYA). Pavel Petrovich Shcherbuk, retired cornet of the guards!

SHCHERBUK. Yes, yes . . . and the rest?

ANNA. Ah, yes, of course . . . Our friend, neighbour, guest and creditor.

SHCHERBUK. Indeed yes! Closest friend of His Excellency, the late General! Under his command stormed the forts known as the fair sextet. (*He bows.*) Pray be so good, your hand . . .

SOFYA (*holding out her hand, then pulling it back*). Charmed . . . but it's not necessary.

SHCHERBUK. I'm hurt, Ma'am! Carried your husband about in my arms when he was still walking round under the table . . . I bear a mark from him, a mark that I'll carry with me to my grave. (*He opens his mouth.*) There! There's a tooth missing, do you see? (*Everyone laughs.*) I was holding him in my arms and he, the little imp, wielding the pistol with which he was deigning to amuse himself, proceeded to administer me a correction right here on the teeth! Your loveliness reminds me of a certain picture, only the nose isn't quite the same . . . Will you not let me have your hand?

PETRIN *sits next to* ABRAM VENGEROVICH *and reads the newspaper aloud to him.*

SOFYA (*extending her hand*). If you must . . .

SHCHERBUK (*kissing her hand*). Merci to you! (*To* PLATONOV.) Well, Míshenka, and what a fine figure of a man you've grown to be, eh? A beauty, isn't he, eh? And why don't you join the army, my cupid?

PLATONOV. I've a weak chest, Pavel Petrovich.

SHCHERBUK (*pointing to* NIKOLAI TRILETSKI). Did he tell you that? Believe that chatterbox and you'll find yourself without a head on your shoulders!

NIKOLAI TRILETSKI. I'll trouble you to mind your language, Pavel Petrovich!

SHCHERBUK. He treated me for a backache . . . Don't eat this, don't eat that. Didn't cure me. So I asked him 'What do you take my money for if you can't cure me?' To which he says: 'Either one or the other, he says, either you cure, or you take money.' How do you like that?

NIKOLAI TRILETSKI. Why tell fibs, Beelzebub Bucephalovich? Six calls and I only got one rouble, and a torn one at that. I was going to give it to a beggar, but even he wouldn't take it. 'Badly torn,' he said, 'the numbers are missing.'

SHCHERBUK. Six calls you made, not because of my backache, but because of my tenant's daughter that's quelque chose.

NIKOLAI TRILETSKI. Platonov, you're sitting near him, give him a good clip on his bald pate on my behalf!

SHCHERBUK. Keep off! That'll do! Don't tease a sleeping lion! (*To* PLATONOV.) And your father was a fine fellow too! Great friends we were! . . . (*To* PETRIN.) Gerasya! Is nothing sacred to you? Here we are holding a conversation and you read your newspaper aloud! Have some manners!

PETRIN *continues to read.* IVAN TRILETSKI *dozes;* SASHA *nudges him; he wakes, but drops off again in a minute.*

One can't talk! (*He rises.*) Listen to him! He goes on reading!

PETRIN (*rising and coming up to* PLATONOV). What did you say, sir?

PLATONOV. Nothing at all . . .

PETRIN. No, you said something. Something about Petrin . . . Criticising . . .

PLATONOV. You must have been dreaming, I assure you. I said nothing.

PETRIN. You can say as much as you like! Petrin! Petrin! What is Petrin? (*He puts the newspaper into his pocket.*) Perhaps Petrin went to a university. Did you know that? Yes, and perhaps he's a doctor of law. Did you know that? That's how it is . . . And I've lived a little longer than you . . . Approaching my sixtieth year, thank God.

PLATONOV. Very nice, I'm sure, but what does it prove?

PETRIN. Live to my age, sweetheart, you'll know! Life's no joke! It bites, it hurts . . .

PLATONOV. I really don't know what you're getting at! You start off with yourself, then you go on to life. What is there in common between you and life?

PETRIN. Life, my dear sir . . . What is life? I'll tell you what it is! When man is born into this world, he takes one of the three roads of life open before him: go to the right and you're eaten up by the wolves; go to the left and *you* eat up the wolves; go straight ahead and you eat yourself up . . .

PLATONOV. Just fancy that! Hm . . . And did you reach this conclusion by means of research, experience?

PETRIN. Experience!

PLATONOV. Experience! (*He laughs.*) My dear Gerasim Kuzmich, tell all this to somebody else, only don't tell me. Friends of my father, in all sincerity, I simply do not believe in your ancient, home-grown wisdom . . .

PORFIFI GLAGOLYEV (*extending his hand*). My dear boy, thank you for your sincerity! It binds me to you all the closer!

ANNA. I don't care for such conversations, especially when they're conducted by Platonov. They always end unpleasantly . . . Mikhail Vasilyevich, let me introduce our new friend! (*She indicates* ISAK VENGEROVICH.) Isak Abramovich Vengerovich who's a student . . .

PLATONOV. Ah . . . (*He rises and goes up to* ISAK VENGEROVICH.) How do you do! (*He offers his hand.*) What wouldn't I give to have the right to call myself a student again . . . (*There is a pause.*) I'm offering you my hand. . . Take it or give me yours . . .

ISAK VENGEROVICH. I shall do neither one nor the other.

PLATONOV. Really! How enigmatic! Why not?

ANNA (*aside*). Hell!

ISAK VENGEROVICH. I have grounds enough. I despise such people as you.

PLATONOV. Bravissimo! (*Looking him over.*) I'd say I was terribly pleased, if I didn't feel that it would be flattering your vanity dangerously! (*There is a pause.*) You look at me as though you were a giant and I a pygmy. Perhaps you really are a giant?

ISAK VENGEROVICH. I'm an honest man, not a vulgar oaf.

PLATONOV. I congratulate you . . . But no one is calling your honesty into question . . . Won't you let me have your hand, young man?

ISAK VENGEROVICH. I don't give alms.

NIKOLAI TRILETSKI *lets out a whistle.*

PLATONOV. That's your affair. I'm talking about manners, not alms. Do you despise me very much?

ISAK VENGEROVICH. As much as it is possible for one who with all his heart and soul hates vulgarity, parasites and buffoons . . .

PLATONOV (*sighing*). I haven't heard such speeches for a long time now. I used to be quite expert in them too . . . Only, unfortunately, they're only phrases, that's all . . . Just a little drop of sincerity would help . . . False notes jar terribly on the unaccustomed ear . . .

ISAK VENGEROVICH. Wouldn't it be better for us to break off this conversation?

PLATONOV. Why? Our audience is willing . . . Let's carry on in the same vein . . .

VASILI *runs in followed by* OSIP.

OSIP. It's an honour and a pleasure to welcome Your Excellency back home. (*A short pause.*) I wish you everything that you wish of God! (*Everyone laughs.*)

ANNA. Well, I declare! Now the party's really complete! What have you come for?

OSIP. To welcome you back home, Your Excellency!

ANNA. I needed that badly, I must say! Get out with you!

PLATONOV. It's a long time since I saw you last, murderer No 666!

ANNA. Don't hold him back, Platonov, let him go! I'm angry with him! (*To* OSIP.) Tell them in the kitchen to give you something to eat. Just look at those bestial eyes! How much wood did you steal over the winter, eh?

OSIP. May I have your hand to kiss?

ANNA (*lifting her hand to his lips*). There, kiss it!

OSIP. I'm very grateful to Your Excellency for your kindness! (*He bows.*) Why are you holding on to me Mikhail Vasilyevich?

PLATONOV. Afraid that you might go. I like you, dear fellow! The devil take you, you great brute! Look, ladies and gentlemen, here we have one of the interesting bloodthirsty specimens from our contemporary zoological museum! (*He turns* OSIP *round to face all sides.*) Known to all and sundry as Osip, horse-thief, parasite, murderer and burglar. Born in Vóinitsevka, stole and murdered in Vóinitsevka and bound to perish here in this same Vóinitsevka! (*There is general laughter.*)

NIKOLAI TRILETSKI (*examining him*). What's your job, my good man?

OSIP. Thieving.

PLATONOV. He's smiling, oh ye gods! What a smile! And the face, the face! There's a ton of iron in that face! (*Moving him over to a mirror.*) Look at yourself, monster! What do you see?

OSIP. Just an ordinary man. Even less . . .

PLATONOV. The strength of him! These aren't muscles, they're steel cables! By the way, why aren't you in Siberia?

Everyone laughs.

OSIP. Well now, the law says you only go to Siberia when there's circumstantial evidence or if you're caught committing the crime. Of course, everyone knows that I'm a thief and a brigand (*he laughs*) but not everyone can prove it. No. The peasants are a lot of cowards nowadays, they're stupid. Scared of everything. Scared to prove anything too. They could have me exiled, but they don't understand the law. 'Fraid of everything. Trashy people, not worth spitting on! I don't feel sorry for hurting them.

PLATONOV. There's reasoning for you! And he's thought it all up himself, the repulsive beast! And it's all based on theories! (*He sighs.*) Such vile filth still possible in Russia!

OSIP. I'm not the only one, Mikhail Vasilyevich. Everyone thinks that way. Now there's Abram Abramovich here . . .

He points to ABRAM VENGEROVICH.

PLATONOV. But he's outside the law too! 'All know, but none can prove.'

ABRAM VENGEROVICH. I think, perhaps, it'd be better if you left me alone.

PLATONOV. There's nothing to choose between you, only he has sixty pubs.

ABRAM VENGEROVICH. Sixty-three pubs.

PLATONOV. It'll be seventy-three in a year's time! He has his charities, dinners, everyone respects him, they bow and scrape . . .

ABRAM VENGEROVICH. You're letting your imagination run away with you, Mikhail Vasilyevich. (*He gets up and goes and sits on another chair.*)

PLATONOV. And when he dies, it'll be in peace and comfort . . .

ANNA. Stop it, Platonov!

ABRAM VENGEROVICH. He wants to drive me away from here, but he won't succeed.

PLATONOV. I'll succeed! I'll succeed or I'll go myself!

ANNA. Platonov! Are you going to stop or not?

SASHA. For Heaven's sake! (*In a quiet voice.*) So rude! You're putting me to shame!

PLATONOV (*to* OSIP). Go on, get to hell out of here!

OSIP. Marfa Petrovna has a parrot and whenever it sees a man or a dog, it calls them fools, but the moment it catches sight of Mr. Vengerovich, it yells out 'Hell and damnation!' (*He goes out.*)

ABRAM VENGEROVICH. If anyone's going to lecture me on morality, young man, it's not going to be you, and least of all in such a way. I'm a citizen and, if the truth be told, I'm a useful citizen. I'm a father. And who are you? Just who are you, young man? Begging your pardon, you're just a fop, a spendthrift, a penniless landowner! You're a depraved man; you've no right at all to the sacred task that you've undertaken.

PLATONOV. That everyone should kowtow to this fattened, gilded parvenu! That all sense of honour should be thrown on to the dust heap! Citizen! If you're a citizen, then 'citizen's' a swear word!

ANNA. Platonov! Platonov, you're starting last year's business all over again and I will not put up with it!

PLATONOV (*taking a drink of water*). All right. (*He sits down.*)

ABRAM VENGEROVICH. All right. (*There is a pause.*)

SHCHERBUK. I'm a martyr, my friends, a martyr!

ANNA. Now what?

SHCHERBUK. Better to be in one's grave than live with a malicious wife! She nearly killed me last week with that devil, that red-headed Don Juan of hers! They fell on me, both of them, as I was taking my nap in the garden last week! They beat me mercilessly . . .

ANNA. You must be exaggerating, Pavel Petrovich!

SHCHERBUK. I assure you . . . I thought it was an upheaval of the elements, the universal flood, the rain of fire! And just think of it, she's the most ancient hag in the world, the old fright, and there she is with a lover! Oh, the witch! Suits that red-head of a Don Juan, of course, it's her money he's . . .

YAKOV *meanwhile enters and hands* ANNA *a card.*

ANNA (*reading*). 'Comte Glagolief'. Why this ceremony? Show him in, please. (*To* PORFIRI GLAGOLYEV.) It's your son, Porfiri Semyonovich!

PORFIRI GLAGOLYEV. My son? How can he be here? He's abroad!

Enter KIRIL GLAGOLYEV.

ANNA. Kiril Porfiryevich! How kind!

PORFIRI GLAGOLYEV (*rising*). You, Kiril . . . You're back? (*He sits down again.*)

KIRIL GLAGOLYEV. How do you do, mesdames! Platonov, Vengerovich, Triletski. And funny old Platonov here too! How terribly hot it is in Russia! I've come straight from Paris! Now that's a city! . . . No, no, it's just . . . just my father I must see. (*To his father.*) Look here, what's all this about? Why didn't you send me the money as I asked?

PORFIRI GLAGOLYEV. We'll talk about it at home.

KIRIL GLAGOLYEV. Why didn't you send me the money? Is it a joke? Ladies and gentlemen, how can one live abroad without money?

ANNA. Tell us all about Paris. Do sit down, Kiril Porfiryevich!

KIRIL GLAGOLYEV. Thanks to him, I returned with nothing but a toothpick! Thirty-five telegrams I sent him from Paris! Why didn't you send me the money, I ask you? So you're blushing, eh? Ashamed?

PORFIRI GLAGOLYEV. Don't make a scene, Kiril! I thought that six thousand would be enough.

KIRIL GLAGOLYEV. Give me the money now, I'm going back! Give it to me! I'm in a hurry!

YAKOV (*entering*). Lunch is on the table.

With a loud whoop NIKOLAI TRILETSKI *seizes* SASHA *with one arm and* KIRIL GLAGOLYEV *with the other and rushes them to the door.*

SASHA. Let go of me, you madcap! I'll go myself!

KIRIL GLAGOLYEV. Let me go! What impudence! Can't stand all this horseplay! (*He tears himself away.*)

ANNA (*leading* KIRIL GLAGOLYEV). Come, monsieur le

parisien! Why worry over trifles? Abram Abramovich, Timofei Gordeyevich, please! (*She goes out with* KIRIL GLAGOLYEV.)

BUGROV *stretches himself and goes out, followed by* ABRAM *and* ISAK VENGEROVICH.

PLATONOV (*offering his arm to* SOFYA). Still unknown to you, this little world! A world of utter, hopeless fools . . . (*He goes out with* SOFYA.)

ABRAM VENGEROVICH (*to his son*). Did you see that?

ISAK VENGEROVICH. An extraordinary scoundrel! (*He goes out with his father.*)

VOINITSEV (*nudging* IVAN TRILETSKI). Ivan Ivanovich! Ivan Ivanovich! Lunch!

IVAN TRILETSKI (*jumping up*). Eh? Who?

VOINITSEV. No one. Come and have lunch!

IVAN TRILETSKI. Very well, my pet! (*They go out with* VOINITSEV *and* SHCHERBUK.)

PORFIRI GLAGOLYEV. I've nothing against it, as I've told you, but will she . . .

PETRIN. Of course she will! Lord smite me! Of course she will! Would you like me to have a talk with her?

PORFIRI GLAGOLYEV. No. I'm perfectly capable of getting married without anyone's help. (*He goes out.*)

PETRIN (*alone*). If only he could! Holy saints, put yourselves in my position! If the widow marries him, I'm a rich man! (ANNA *enters.*) Dear Anna Petrovna, may I drop a hint?

ANNA. Do, by all means, only be quick please . . . I've no time . . .

PETRIN. M-m. Couldn't you let me have a little money, Anna Petrovna?

ANNA. You call that a hint? How much do you want? One rouble, two roubles?

PETRIN. It's those bills of exchange, I mean. I'm so sick of looking at them! They're only a delusion, that's all . . .

ANNA. Is it still that sixteen thousand you're talking about? Aren't you ashamed? Have you no conscience? What does an old bachelor like you want with that unclean money?

PETRIN. I want it because it's mine, dear lady.

ANNA. You wheedled those bills of exchange out of my husband when he was sick and drunk. Do you remember that? Enough! I've no money myself and there's none for you! Off with you! (*She goes to the door.*) Go and tuck into your lunch!

PETRIN. Just one second! Tell me, dear lady, do you like Porfiri?

ANNA. And what business is it of yours? Eh, advocate? You and your jurisprudence, you! (PLATONOV *enters.*)

PETRIN. What business is it of mine? (*Beating his breast.*) And who, permit me to ask you, was the closest friend of the late general? Who closed his eyes on his death bed?

ANNA. You, you, you! And you were a real brick to have done it!

PETRIN (*sighing*). You're a proud woman, milady! A deadly sin, pride! (*He goes out.*)

PLATONOV (*kissing her hand*). I want to drive them all out of here!

ANNA. Insufferable Mikhail Vasilyevich. Think how much *I* want to shoo them all out of the house! Our trouble is that neither I nor your eloquence have the right to shoo them out! They're our benefactors, our creditors . . . We could be out of the estate tomorrow! So you see my dear chatterbox, if you don't want me to leave these delightful halls, just don't touch my gaggle of geese! They're calling me. We'll be going for a drive after dinner. Don't you dare leave! (*She slaps him on the shoulder.*) Our turn will come! Come and eat! (*She goes out.*)

PLATONOV (*after a pause*). Nevertheless, I'll drive him out! I'll shoo them all out! It's stupid, it's tactless, but I'll do it . . .

Enter ISAK VENGEROVICH.

ISAK VENGEROVICH. Listen, Mister Schoolmaster, I strongly advise you to leave my father alone.

PLATONOV. Merci for the advice.

ISAK VENGEROVICH. I'm not joking. My father has many connections and could easily have you removed from your post. I warn you.

PLATONOV. Magnanimous youth! What's your name?

ISAK VENGEROVICH. Isak.

PLATONOV. So, Abraham begat Isak! Thanks, magnanimous youth! And would you take the trouble to tell your papa from me that I desire the earth to swallow him up together with his many minions! Go and eat, youth, or there'll be nothing left for you!

ISAK VENGEROVICH (*shrugging his shoulders and going to the door*). Do you think I'm angry with you because you keep on pestering my father? Not a bit of it! I'm not angry, I just study you . . . and I understand you! Believe me, if it weren't for the boredom induced by your sheer idleness, you'd never even notice my father. It's not truth that you seek, it's amusement, diversion. Now that you've lost all your menials, you must find someone to scold. And so you scold all and sundry.

PLATONOV (*laughing*). That's fine, by God! Do you know, I think you're not without a little intelligence!

ISAK VENGEROVICH. What is remarkable is that you never quarrel with my father tête-à-tête; you always make sure there's an audience in the drawing-room to admire you in all your majesty! Man of the theatre!

PLATONOV. I'd like to have a talk with you in ten years' time, or even five. Will you keep that sparkle in your eye, that tone of voice? It all goes off, young man, it all fades. However, go and eat. I'm not going to talk to you any more. I don't care for that malicious visage of yours!

ISAK VENGEROVICH (*laughing*). Aesthete! (*He goes to the door.*) Better a malicious visage than one that asks to be slapped.

PLATONOV. I daresay . . . Go and eat!

ISAK VENGEROVICH. We don't know each other . . . Please don't forget that! (*He goes out.*)

PLATONOV (*alone*). Ignorant, loquacious youth! (*Left alone, he looks through the door into the dining-room.*) She's looking from side to side. Looking for me with those velvet eyes of hers! How pretty she still is! And the same hair! Same colour, wears it in the same way! How many times I kissed that hair! (*A pause.*) Have I reached the age when the only joy left is in memories? (*A pause.*) Is it . . . the end? Heaven forbid! I must live . . . live! I'm still young!

Enter VOINITSEV.

VOINITSEV (*wiping his lips with his napkin*). Come and drink to Sophie's health! Why are you hiding, eh? What is it?

PLATONOV. I'm admiring your wife! Miraculous! You're a lucky man!

VOINITSEV. Yes, I know, I know! (*He laughs. They both look through the door.*)

PLATONOV (*laughing*). And there's my little Sasha, my little peasant wench! Look at her! Still indignant at my behaviour! Furious with me!

VOINITSEV. Forgive a personal question . . . Are you happy with her?

PLATONOV. It's a family, my friend! Take her away and it'd be the end of me! A nest! You'll find out! And it's a perfect match: she's stupid and I'm good-for-nothing! Couldn't be better!

Enter NIKOLAI TRILETSKI.

NIKOLAI TRILETSKI. Come on mateys. (*He embraces them*

both at the same time.) Let's go and drink to the happy homecoming! Ooogh! (*He stretches himself.*)

PLATONOV (*to* VOINITSEV). Tell me, what's the meaning of the notice in the paper today? Has the time really come?

VOINITSEV. No, don't worry! (*Laughing.*) It's just a little financial dodge. There'll be an auction and Glagolyev will buy the estate. We'll just pay the mortgage off to him instead of the bank. It's his idea.

PLATONOV. I don't understand. What does he stand to gain? Is he making a present of it or what?

VOINITSEV. I don't really understand it myself. Ask Mama, she'll explain it all. (*Takes* PLATONOV *by the arm.*) Come . . . Come Nikolai Ivanovich. (*Taking* NIKOLAI TRILETSKI *by the arm.*) Let's go and drink to our eternal friendship . . .

ANNA (*appearing at the door*). There's friendship for you! A find troika! (*She sings.*) 'Shall I harness a swift troika . . .'

NIKOLAI TRILETSKI (*taking up the tune*) '. . . of brown horses dark and free . . .' Come on boys, we start with the brandy!

ANNA (*standing at the door*). Come on, you spongers, come and eat! It's all cold!

PLATONOV. Ah, there's friendship for you! I've always been lucky in love, but unlucky in friendship. I'm afraid that my friendship may bring you tears. Let's drink to the happy outcome of all friendships, including ours! May its end be as peaceful and gentle as its beginning! (*They go into the dining-room.*)

Curtain

Act Two

SCENE ONE

The garden. In the foreground there is a flower-bed with a pathway encircling it. In the middle of the flower-bed stands a statue with a lampion on its head. Round about there are benches, chairs and small tables. To the right one can see the façade of the house with its porch. The windows are open; through them can be heard laughter, conversation and the sounds of a piano and violin playing quadrilles, waltzes, etc. Farther into the garden can be seen a Chinese summer-house festooned with lanterns. Above the doorway of the summer-house is a monogram with the letters 'S.V.' Beyond the summer-house a game of skittles is in progress: one can hear the sound of the balls rolling and appropriate exclamations: 'Five!' 'Four!' etc. Both house and garden are illuminated. Guests and servants scurry about the garden. VASILI *and* YAKOV *in tails, both of them drunk, are hanging up lanterns and lighting lampions.*

NIKOLAI TRILETSKI, *in a peak-cap with a cockade, enters from the house arm-in-arm with* BUGROV.

NIKOLAI TRILETSKI. . . . You can afford it! I'm only asking for a loan . . .

BUGROV. God's my witness, I can't, Nikolai Ivanovich!

NIKOLAI TRILETSKI. You can, Timofei Gordeyevich! You could hold up the entire universe to ransom, only you don't want to! It's only a loan, don't you see, you extraordinary fellow! Word of honour, you won't get it back!

BUGROV. You see, you see? You've let the cat out of the bag . . .

NIKOLAI TRILETSKI. I don't see anything! All I see is your hard-heartedness! Come, give, oh you great man! . . .

BUGROV (*sighing*). E-heh-eh! Nikolai Ivanovich! When it comes to curing a sick man, you're not up to much, but you still go on squeezing out money . . . (*Opening his wallet.*) It's for the last time, Nikolai Ivanovich. (*Counting.*) One . . . six . . . twelve . . .

NIKOLAI TRILETSKI (*looking into the wallet*). Gracious me! And then they go and say that Russians don't have any money nowadays! Where did you rake up that little collection?

BUGROV. Fifty . . . (*Handing him the money.*) It's for the last time . . .

NIKOLAI TRILETSKI. And what's this little note here? You give me that one too. It's looking at me so tenderly! (*Taking the money.*) And that one!

BUGROV (*giving him more*). Take it! There's greed in you a-plenty, Nikolai Ivanovich!

NIKOLAI TRILETSKI. Nothing but one rouble notes! Have you been begging at the church door, or what? They're not counterfeit, by any chance?

BUGROV. Let's have them back then, if they're counterfeit!

NIKOLAI TRILETSKI. Have you got a lot of money, Timofei Gordeyevich?

BUGROV. Enough to see me through.

NIKOLAI TRILETSKI. You rogue! Why are you buying up the Voinitsev bills, eh?

BUGROV. It's not the kind of thing you'd understand, Nikolai Ivanovich!

NIKOLAI TRILETSKI. So you and Vengerovich want to snap up Her Excellency's mines, do you? She'll take pity on her step-son, won't she? She won't let him perish, she'll give you her mines, won't she? You're a great man, but you're a rogue, a cheat.

BUGROV. Now look, Nikolai Ivanovich . . . I'm going to take

a little nap near the summer-house, so wake me up, will you, when supper's ready.

NIKOLAI TRILETSKI. Lovely, lovely! Go and sleep!

BUGROV (*going*). And if they're not going to give us any supper, wake me up at half past ten. (*He goes off towards the summer-house.*)

NIKOLAI TRILETSKI (*examining the money*). Smells of peasant! What a pile, the dirty dog! What am I going to do with it all? (*To* VASILI *and* YAKOV.) Hey, you, the gentlemen volunteers! Vasili, call Yakov over here! Yakov, call Vasili over here! Come on, crawl over here to me! Look sharp!

YAKOV *and* VASILI *come up to* NIKOLAI TRILETSKI.

NIKOLAI TRILETSKI. They're in tails! Damn me, but you look like your masters. (*Giving* YAKOV *a rouble.*) There's a rouble for you. (*To* VASILI.) There's a rouble for you. That's for having long noses, both of you!

YAKOV *and* VASILI (*bowing*). Very much obliged to you, Nikolai Ivanovich!

NIKOLAI TRILETSKI. Oh, but ye Slavs, why are you swaying about? Pickled, eh? (*He gives them another rouble each.*) There's another rouble each for you! That's because you're called Yakov and he Vasili and not the other way round! Go on, bow! (*They bow.*) Quite right! And here's another rouble each for you, because I'm called Nikolai Ivanovich and not Ivan Nikolayevich! Bow! That's it!

VOINITSEV *passes.*

NIKOLAI TRILETSKI (*to* VOINITSEV). Here you are, three roubles for you!

VOINITSEV *pockets the money absent-mindedly and goes off into the depths of the garden.*

NIKOLAI TRILETSKI. Well, say 'thank you' then!

IVAN TRILETSKI *and* SASHA *come out of the house.*

SASHA. Oh my God, when is all this going to end? This one's drunk, Nikolai's drunk, and Misha too! Everyone's looking at you, you shameless creatures! And what about me? Do you think I enjoy seeing everyone point at you?

IVAN TRILETSKI. Wait, wait! That's not it! You've got me all muddled up! What was I saying? Yes! No, I'm not lying, my dear! Had I served another five years I would have been a general!

SASHA. Come along! Generals don't drink like that!

IVAN TRILETSKI. Everyone drinks for joy! I'd be a general! Oh, do be quiet as a special favour! Exactly like her mother! Z-z-z-z . . . Lord God almighty! Her mother would be at it day and night, day and night! This isn't so and that isn't so! Z-z-z-z . . . What was I saying? Yes! And you're exactly like your late mother! Exactly! Eyes, hair! And she walked the same way, too, like a goose! (*He kisses her.*) How I loved her, your poor mother!

NIKOLAI TRILETSKI. Here you are, your lordship, here's a hundred copecks for you! (*He gives him a rouble.*)

IVAN TRILETSKI. C'est ça! I accept it, my son, merci! I wouldn't take it from a stranger, but from my son . . . I do dislike other people's finances, my little ones!

NIKOLAI TRILETSKI (*to* SASHA). Shall I give you some too? Well, here's some for you too! Three roubles for you! Three roubles . . .

SASHA. Give me two more while you're about it. I'll buy some material for Misha's summer trousers, he's only got one pair.

NIKOLAI TRILETSKI. I wouldn't give him any kind of trousers if I had any say in the matter! Here you are then!

IVAN TRILETSKI. What was I saying? Yes . . . I remember it is as though it were today . . . Ah yes . . . I was at Main H.Q. I used my head against the enemy, I spilt Turkish blood with my brains. Never held a bayonet, no, never . . .

Ah yes . . . Innocent of that, thank God!

SASHA. Come along now, it's time! Good-bye Kolya! Come on, Papa!

IVAN TRILETSKI. Keep quiet, for pity's sake! Chirp, chirp, chirp! just like a starling! Yes, that's the way to live, my children! Honourably, decently! Yes, yes . . . I was awarded the Cross of St. Vladimir, third class . . .

SASHA. That's enough, Papa! Come along now . . .

NIKOLAI TRILETSKI. We know what kind of a man you are without you holding forth . . . Off with you now, see her home!

SASHA. You've got his cap, Kolya. Give it to him or he'll catch a chill . . .

ANNA PETROVNA *appears at a window.*

NIKOLAI TRILETSKI (*taking off the cap and putting it on his father's head*). About turn!

IVAN TRILETSKI. Le-e-e-ft i-i-in-n-cline! Yes, yes! Yes, yes! You're a good man, Nikolai, Heaven knows you are! Come on, Sasha! Are you coming? Here, let me carry you! I always used to carry your mother about. Once I came crashing down off a hillock together with her. All she did was to burst out laughing, the darling. She wasn't angry at all. Come on, let me carry you!

SASHA. The idea! What next? Straighten your cap. (*She does so.*) A fine fellow you are!

IVAN TRILETSKI. Ah yes, ah yes . . . (*They go out.*)

Enter PETRIN *and* SHCHERBUK *from the house.*

PETRIN (*arm-in-arm with* SHCHERBUK). Just put fifty thousand in front of me, and I'd steal them! Word of honour, I'd steal them! Put them in front of you and you'd steal them too . . .

SHCHERBUK. I wouldn't steal them, Gerasya, no!

PETRIN. Just put one rouble down in front of me, and I'd

steal the rouble! Honesty! Pooh! Who wants your honesty? If a fellow's an honest man, it means he's a fool . . .

SHCHERBUK. Then I'm a fool! All right, I'm a fool . . .

NIKOLAI TRILETSKI. Here you are, venerable sirs, here's a rouble each for you! (*He gives each a rouble.*)

PETRIN (*taking it*). Hand it over . . .

SHCHERBUK (*laughs and takes the money*). Merci, monsier le docteur!

ANNA PETROVNA (*from the window*). Triletski! Give me a rouble too! (*She disappears.*)

NIKOLAI TRILETSKI. For you, not just a rouble, but five roubles, madam the major-general's widow! Coming! (*He goes into the house.*)

PETRIN. Can't bear her! Bad woman! Too much pride! (*He shakes his head.*) Have you seen Glagolyev? There's a goggle-eyed dummy for you! Sits there like a toadstool! Courting!

SHCHERBUK. He'll marry her!

PETRIN. If only he would! But when? In a hundred years' time? Lord! Look, since the old general died, God rest his soul, they've absolutely nothing left. She's got the mines still, but Vengerovich has his eyes on them, and who am I to compete with Vengerovich? What could I get for my bills now? If I protest them now, what would I get?

SHCHERBUK. Nihil.

PETRIN. But if she marries Glagolyev, then I'll know who to get it off! He'll come to his step-son's rescue, he'll pay up! (*He sighs.*) Think of it! Sixteen thousand, Pavochka!

SHCHERBUK. And three thousand to me . . . My old battle-axe orders me to go and collect . . . How can I collect? They're not peasants, they're friends. Let her come here herself and collect! Come on, Gerasya, let's go to the servants' wing! We'll whisper sweet ballads to the ladies' sextet.

PETRIN. Is Dunyasha there?

SHCHERBUK. She's there. (*They move off.*) It's gayer there! (*He sings.*) 'Sad am I that therein do I dwell no more . . .'

PETRIN. Tic-toc, tic-toc . . . (*He shouts.*) Yes sir! (*Singing.*) 'Merrily we see the New Year in, true friends together we drink to him . . .' (*They go out.*)

Enter VOINITSEV *and* SOFYA *from the depths of the garden.*

VOINITSEV. What are you thinking of?

SOFYA. Really, I don't know. (*They sit.*) Don't pay any attention to my moods. (*A pause.*) Let's go away from here, Sergei!

VOINITSEV. Go away from here?

SOFYA. Yes.

VOINITSEV. Why?

SOFYA. I want to . . . Even abroad. Shall we? . . . I like it here, it's gay, the air's wholesome, but I just can't . . . Everything is going very well, only . . . we must go! You gave your word not to ask me why.

VOINITSEV. We'll leave tomorrow! (*He kisses her hand.*) You're bored here. How I understand you! God knows what kind of a milieu we have here! Petrins, Shcherbuks . . .

SOFYA. They're not to blame . . . Let's forget about them . . .

A pause.

VOINITSEV. Where do you women get all your melancholy from? (*He kisses her on the cheek.*) Enough! Cheer up! Live, while you have life in you! Can't you send your melancholy packing, as Platonov puts it? Have a good, heart-to-heart chat with him! He'll conjure your melancholy away for you! And you ought to talk with maman more often, and with Triletski. (*Laughing.*) They're people after my own heart. You'll like them too when you get to know them better.

ANNA (*appearing at a window*). Sergei! Sergei! Hey there! Call Sergei Pavlovich!

VOINITSEV. What can I do for you?

ANNA. You're there? Come here a minute!

VOINITSEV. Coming! (*To* SOFYA.) We leave tomorrow, unless you change your mind! (*He goes into the house.*)

SOFYA (*after a pause*). Why, it's almost tragic! Already I'm capable of not thinking of my husband for days on end, of not noticing his presence, of not paying any attention to what he says . . . What am I to do? (*She thinks.*) The wedding was such a short time ago and already . . . And it's all that – Platonov! I haven't the force, I haven't the strength of character to withstand this man! He pursues me from morning to night, he seeks me, he gives me no rest with those all-seeing eyes of his! He has only to take one step and anything might happen! . . .

PLATONOV *comes out of the house.*

PLATONOV. It's hot! Shouldn't drink . . . (*He sees* SOFYA.) You here, Sofya Yegorovna! In solitary splendour? (*He laughs.*)

SOFYA. Yes!

PLATONOV. You flee mortals? (*He sits down beside her.*) May I? (*A pause.*) I'm glad that at long last we can talk. You avoid me, you walk the other way, you don't look at me. What is this? Comedy, or in earnest? Is it my fault? Do I repel you? (*He stands up.*)

SOFYA. I admit I . . . have been avoiding you . . . a little . . . Had I known it was so unpleasant for you, I would have conducted affairs otherwise . . .

PLATONOV. You avoid me? You admit it? (*He sits down.*) But . . . why? To what end?

SOFYA. Don't shout, I mean, don't talk so loudly! This is not, I trust, a reprimand. I don't like people shouting at me! Strictly speaking it's not you that I've been avoiding, but conversations with you. Hardly a day passes without your telling me how once you loved me, how I loved you and so forth. Undergraduate loves girl, girl loves undergraduate . . . The tale is too old and commonplace to be worth so much re-telling or for us to attach any significance to it now. Then you seem to be asking for something, as if then, in the past, you had'nt quite finished helping yourself to something that you would like to have now. You appear to attach far too great a significance . . . how can I put it more clearly? . . . you exaggerate our relationship as good friends! There's something strange in the way you look, the way you lose your temper, shout, seize me by the hand, pursue me . . . (*A pause.*)

PLATONOV. Is that all? (*He stands up.*) Merci for being so frank! (*He goes to the door.*)

SOFYA (*standing up*). Mikhail Vasilyevich! Why take umbrage? I didn't . . .

PLATONOV (*stopping*). A nice one, you are! (*A pause.*) So then, it's not that you're tired of me, but that you're afraid of me, that you're funking it! Are you funking it, Sofya Yegorovna? (*He approaches her*).

SOFYA. Stop it, Platonov! You're lying! I have not been, nor do I intend to be afraid!

PLATONOV. And where's your strength of character, where's that sober intellect of yours, if every man you meet who happens to be in the slightest degree above the banal seems to you to constitute a danger for your Sergei Pavlovich? I talked with you because I considered you an intelligent, understanding woman! What profound depravity!

SOFYA. No one gave you the right to say such things!

PLATONOV (*laughing*). Pursued? Sought, grabbed by the hands? Poor thing! Does he want to take you away from your husband? Is he in love with you? Platonov in love with you? Ce fou de Platonov? What luck! Absolute bliss!

He goes into the house.

SOFYA. You're impertinent and rude, Platonov! You've gone

mad! (*She follows him and stops at the door.*) It's terrible! Why did he say all that? He wanted to sweep me off my feet . . . No, I will not put up with it! I'll go and tell him . . .

She goes into the house.

OSIP *comes out from behind the summer-house.*

OSIP (*to* YAKOV). What's his name? m-m-m . . . . Vengerovich . . . Go and call him! Quietly! Tell him it's important . . .

YAKOV. All right. (*He goes into the house.*)

OSIP *tears down a lantern, blows it out and pockets it. He then tears down another lantern and repeats the process.*

VASILI. They're not for you to pull down, the lanterns . . .

OSIP. Well, look who's here! How's things, horseface? (*He takes* VASILI'S *cap and throws it up into a tree.*) Go on, smack my face for being a bad man! (*Pause.*) Want to kill me, don't you? Go on, kill me then, now, or do you have to go and band up with your artel to do it? Go on, spit, in my face for being a bad man! You won't spit? Afraid of me, are you? All right then, down on your knees! Who do you think I'm talking to, a wall? Down you get!

VASILI (*kneeling*). It's wicked of you, Osip Ivanovich!

ABRAM VENGEROVICH *comes out of the house.*

ABRAM VENGEROVICH. Who's calling me out here?

OSIP (*quickly taking off his cap*). It's me, your worship. The publican said you were wanting me . . .

VASILI *gets up, then sits down on a bench and weeps.*

ABRAM VENGEROVICH. Yes . . . Let's move away a little. (*They move off to a bench upstage.*) Stand a little way apart. Look as though you're not talking to me. That's it. One oughtn't to have anything to do with you . . . You're such an evil fellow . . .

OSIP. Very evil! Worse than anyone else in the world!

ABRAM VENGEROVICH. Don't talk so loudly! The amount of money I've been handing over to you, it's something awful, and you don't feel it at all, as if my money was stones or some other kind of useless article. You allow yourself all kinds of impertinence, you steal . . . You don't like the truth, eh?

OSIP. Was it to hear a sermon you called me here, y'lordship?

ABRAM VENGEROVICH. Not so loud! Do you know . . . Platonov?

OSIP. The teacher? Of course . . .

ABRAM VENGEROVICH. Yes the teacher. The teacher who only teaches swear words and nothing else. How much will you take to cripple him?

OSIP. Cripple him? How do you mean?

ABRAM VENGEROVICH. Not kill, just cripple . . . You shouldn't kill people! . . . Murder – it's such a thing that . . . Cripple him, beat him up so that he'll remember it all his life. Break something . . . some disfigurement on the face . . . What will you take? Sh . . . Someone's coming . . . (*They move farther upstage.*)

PLATONOV *and* GREKOVA *come out of the house.*

PLATONOV (*laughing*). What, what? What did you say? (*He gives a loud laugh.*) I didn't quite catch it . . .

GREKOVA. Well then, I can repeat it. I can express myself even more rudely. Of course, you won't take offence! You're so accustomed to rudeness of all kinds . . .

PLATONOV. Say it, say it, pretty one!

GREKOVA. I am not a pretty one! I'm altogether plain, don't you agree? Frankly now, what's your opinion?

PLATONOV. I'll tell you afterwards. You speak first!

GREKOVA. Then listen! Either you're a man that's completely out of the ordinary or you're a scoundrel. One or the other.

PLATONOV *laughs loudly.*

GREKOVA. You laugh . . . It is funny, too . . . (*She laughs and both of them sit down.*)

PLATONOV (*laughing*). God, what a little ninny! (*Taking her by the waist.*) She philosophises, she does chemistry and what pronouncements she comes out with! (*He kisses her.*) You're a deep one, my pretty little rogue!

GREKOVA. But look . . . What is this? I . . . I didn't say . . . (*She stands up, then sits down.*) Why do you kiss me? I didn't . . .

PLATONOV (*kissing her*). She's in a panic . . . a panic . . . Oh, oh . . .

GREKOVA. Do you . . . do you love me? Yes? . . . Yes?

PLATONOV (*speaking in a squeaking voice*). And do you love me?

GREKOVA. If . . . if . . . then . . . yes . . . (*Weeping.*) Do you love me? Otherwise you wouldn't act like this . . . Do you love me?

PLATONOV. Not a jot, my lovely! I don't love little fools, wicked fellow that I am! She's turned pale! Her eyes flash! She'll show me . . .

GREKOVA (*rising*). You're mocking me, is that it?

A pause.

PLATONOV. For all I know, she'll land me a smack in the face . . .

GREKOVA. I told you, my very dear sir, that either you were an extremely unusual man or a scoundrel, now I tell you that you are an extremely unusual scoundrel! I despise you!

She goes towards the house. NIKOLAI TRILETSKI *enters.*

NIKOLAI TRILETSKI (*wearing a top-hat*). Cranes crying! Where are they from? (*Looking up.*) So soon . . .

GREKOVA. Nikolai Ivanovich, if you have any respect at all

for me . . . for yourself, have nothing to do wth this man! (*She points to* PLATONOV. NIKOLAI TRILETSKI *laughs. She goes into the house.*)

NIKOLAI TRILETSKI (*after a pause*). Eaten her up, brother?

PLATONOV. I haven't eaten anything . . .

NIKOLAI TRILETSKI. It's high time you left her alone, Mikhail Vasilyevich. Really you ought to be ashamed . . .

PLATONOV. Nikolai! What good have you, an intelligent man, found in that little fool?

NIKOLAI TRILETSKI. She's not a fool! She's a victim, that's all. I know, my dear, there are moments when one feels one must hate somebody . . . get your claws into them, play them some dirty little trick. So why not try it on her? She'll do! Weak, dumb, her eyes trusting to the point of stupidity . . .

OSIP (*to* ABRAM VENGEROVICH) . . . and if you don't hand over the rest when the time . . .

ABRAM VENGEROVICH (*to* OSIP). Not so loud! Sh! Off with you. (*He goes towards the house.*)

OSIP *goes off.*

NIKOLAI TRILETSKI. Hell! It's Abram Abramovich! You're not well, are you, Abram Abramovich?

ABRAM VENGEROVICH. I'm very well, thank God!

NIKOLAI TRILETSKI. What a shame! And I need the money so much! Go on, give me some, sweetheart, do!

ABRAM VENGEROVICH. You already owe me a lot, doctor. Two hundred and forty-five roubles, I think.

NIKOLAI TRILETSKI. Lend me some and one day I'll lend you some. Be so kind, magnanimous and brave! The bravest of the Jews is the one that gives a loan without an I.O.U. Be the bravest of the Jews!

ABRAM VENGEROVICH. Hm . . . Always Jews, Jews! I assure you, gentlemen, that in all my life I've never seen a single Russian lend money without an I.O.U., and I assure you that nowhere is the practice of giving money without I.O.U.s so widespread as in dishonest Jewry! There is a lot you young people could learn from us Jews, especially old Jews, very much. We lend you money willingly and you like to laugh at us and make fun of us. That's not good, gentlemen! I'm an old man, I have children. At least consider me a human being. That's why you went to the university. How much? Fifty roubles? (*He takes out his wallet.*)

NIKOLAI TRILETSKI. Lavish! (*Taking the money.*) You're a great man!

ABRAM VENGEROVICH. Doctor, you're wearing my hat!

NIKOLAI TRILETSKI. Yours? Hm . . . (*He takes it off.*) Ought to have it cleaned, you know. They won't charge much! What's the Hebrew for a top-hat? Do you know, it suits you! A regular baron! Why don't you buy yourself a barony?

ABRAM VENGEROVICH. I don't know anything. Why don't you leave me alone? (*He goes into the house.*)

PLATONOV. Why did you take that money from him?

NIKOLAI TRILETSKI. Just took it! Are you sorry for him, or what?

PLATONOV. That's not the point, brother!

NIKOLAI TRILETSKI. What is the point, then?

PLATONOV. You know very well! (*A pause.*) My heart would flame with a mighty love for you, dear friend, if only you'd live just for a week, just for one day, according to some rules, no matter how flimsy . . .

NIKOLAI TRILETSKI. It's not for us, brother, to remodel our flesh! It's not for us to break it! I knew that even back in those days when we used to come bottom of the class in Latin together! So there's no point in chattering about it! (*Pause.*) I was looking at a book the day before yesterday: 'Prominent Men of Today', biographies with portraits. And what do you think? None of us are there; we're just not there! Lasciate ogni speranza, as the Italians say! I could find neither you nor me amongst the top men of today and, just fancy, I'm not worried! Now take Sofya Yegorovna! That's different! She's worried . . .

PLATONOV. And what has Sofya Yegorovna to do with it?

NIKOLAI TRILETSKI. She's hurt that she's not amongst the top men of today . . . She imagines that all she has to do is twitch her little finger and the whole wide world will gape with wonder! She thinks . . . Hm . . . There's more balderdash in her than in all the clever-clever novels you can think of! She's not worth a brass farthing! Ice! Stone! A statue! Sometimes I just feel like going up and scraping the plaster drop off her nose! No strength in her; just a clever doll! Still, judge not lest ye be judged! (*He stands and stretches himself.*) Incidentally, what does the 'S.V.' of that monogram stand for? Sofya Voinitseva or Sergei Voinitsev? Whom did our philologist intend to honour with these symbols, himself or his spouse?

PLATONOV. 'Salve Vengerovich' I'd say. It's his money that's paying for this spree.

NIKOLAI TRILETSKI. Yes . . . What's up with the general's lady today? Laughing, groaning, forcing her kisses on you . . . It's as though she's fallen in love . . .

PLATONOV. Here? Who with? Herself, what? Don't believe her laughter. You can't believe the laughter of a clever woman who never weeps; she laughs when in fact she wants to cry! And today she wants to shoot herself. You can tell by her eyes . . .

NIKOLAI TRILETSKI. Women never shoot themselves, they take poison . . . But let's not philosophise! When I start philosophising I tell the wickedest lies! She's a fine bit of woman, our general's lady! On the whole I have the most terribly bad thoughts when I look at a woman, but not her . . . She's the only one! When I gaze at the practical reality that is her face, well, I begin to believe in platonic love. Let's go and drink. Coming?

PLATONOV. No. It's too close in there.

NIKOLAI TRILETSKI. Oh well . . . I'll have a drink with the priest then. (*He goes off and at the door bumps into* KIRIL GLAGOLYEV.) Ah, Your Illustrious Highness, the home-made count! Here's three roubles for you! (*He thrusts three roubles into his hand and goes into the house.*)

KIRIL GLAGOLYEV. Extraordinary personality! (*Shouting.*) I can give you three roubles myself! Hm . . . Idiot! (*To* PLATONOV.) His stupidity quite astounds me! (*Laughing.*) Hideously stupid! (*He sits down beside* PLATONOV. *Pause.*) How stale the air is in Russia! So dank! I can't stand Russia! The ignorance, the stench, all those ugly snouts putting on their airs and graces . . . Have you never been to Paris?

PLATONOV. Never.

KIRIL GLAGOLYEV. Pity. Still, I suppose you'll manage to get there some time. When you decide to go, do tell me. I'll reveal all the mysteries of Paris to you. I'll give you three hundred letters of introduction and you'll find three hundred of the very chic-est of French cocottes at your disposal.

PLATONOV. Thank you, I've had enough to eat. Tell me, is it true what they say, that your father means to buy the estate?

KIRIL GLAGOLYEV. Really, I don't know. I keep myself far removed from commerce. And have you noticed that mon père is paying court to that general's widow of yours? (*Laughing.*) The old badger wants to get married! The silly goose! And the widow is charmante! Not at all bad-looking! (*Pause.*) And shapely! (*Slapping* PLATONOV *on the back.*) Lucky man! And does she lace herself? Does she?

PLATONOV. I don't know. I'm not there when she dresses . . .

KIRIL GLAGOLYEV. But I was told . . . Aren't you . . .

PLATONOV. Count, you're an idiot.

KIRIL GLAGOLYEV. But I was only joking! Why be angry? Really, what an extraordinary man you are! (*Quietly.*) And is it true that she . . . It's rather a delicate question, but it's just between ourselves, I presume . . . Is it true that sometimes she's ready to cast off everything for love of money?

PLATONOV. That you must ask her yourself. I don't know.

KIRIL GLAGOLYEV. Ask her myself? (*He laughs, then jumps up.*) Upon my word, it's a great idea! Damn it, I'll ask her, Platonov, and I give you my word of honour that she'll be mine! I have a premonition! I'll ask her straight away! I wager you, she's mine! (*He runs to the house and at the door bumps into* ANNA PETROVNA.) Mille pardons, madame! (*He bows repeatedly and goes off.*)

ANNA (*coming over to* PLATONOV). Why are you sitting here?

PLATONOV. It's stuffy inside. I prefer this fine sky to your ceiling.

ANNA (*sitting down*). Wonderful, the weather! The air's pure and cool! Stars in the sky, moon . . . What a pity that ladies can't sleep out under the sky! When I was a little girl, I always used to spend summer nights out in the garden. (*Pause.*) Is that a new tie you've got on?

PLATONOV. It is. (*Pause.*)

ANNA. I'm in some peculiar kind of mood this evening. Everything pleases me . . . Well really, do say something, Platonov! I came out here to hear you speak . . .

PLATONOV. What shall I say to you?

ANNA. Say something to me that's nice and new, nice and pretty, nice and sharp . . . Really, I think that this evening I'm more deeply in love with you than ever before! You're such a darling this evening! Behaving quite well, too!

PLATONOV. And you're looking very beautiful this evening . . . Still, you're always beautiful!

ANNA. Are we friends, you and I, Platonov?

PLATONOV. In all probability . . . I should say, yes, we are friends . . .

ANNA. So we're friends, eh?

PLATONOV. I'd say that we're great friends, after all . . .

ANNA. Great friends?

PLATONOV. What's got into you, my good woman? Friends . . . friends! Just like an old maid!

ANNA. Good! We're friends, and do you know that between a man and a woman from friendship to love is only one step, my very dear sir! (*She laughs.*)

PLATONOV. So that's it? (*He laughs.*) Why say all that? No matter what strides we take, we'll never get as far as hell's door, you and I.

ANNA. Love – hell . . . what a comparison! (*Pause.*) I must have a proper talk with you! It's high time! . . . (*She looks around.*) Please make an effort, mon cher, listen and don't start philosophising!

PLATONOV. Let's go and dance, Anna Petrovna!

ANNA. Let's sit farther off. Come over here. (*She goes and sits down on another bench.*) The only thing is, I don't know where to start! You're such a sluggish, deceitful bit of man meat . . .

PLATONOV. Shall I begin, Anna Petrovna? What I want to say to you is this: why? (*Pause.*) Believe me, better not, Anna Petrovna!

ANNA. But why? Look, listen to me! You don't understand me! If you were free, I would become your wife . . . Well, does silence indicate agreement? Well then? (*Pause.*) Listen, Platonov, in a case like this it's indecent to remain silent!

PLATONOV (*jumping up*). Let's forget this conversation, Anna Petrovna! For God's sake, let's behave as though it never took place! Never!

ANNA (*shrugging her shoulders*). Strange man! But why?

PLATONOV. Because I respect you! Look, my dear friend,

I'm broadminded, I've nothing against having a nice time, I don't oppose having liaisons with women, but . . . but to start up a petty affair with you, a splendid, intelligent woman like you? No! It's too much! To spend a silly month or two together and then to part blushing?

ANNA. We're talking about love!

PLATONOV. And do you think I don't love you? I love you because you are good, intelligent, kind-hearted. I love you desperately, madly! If you want it, I'll lay down my life for you! I love you as a woman, as a human being! Surely we don't have to juggle it so that every kind of love comes to mean *that* kind of love! My love for you is a thousand times more precious to me than the one that's crept into your mind!

ANNA (*standing up*). Go and sleep it off, my dear! Sleep it off and then we'll talk . . .

PLATONOV. Let's forget this conversation! (*He kisses her hand.*) Let's be friends, but no more playing the fool with each other! And don't forget, after all, I am married! Let's forget it all! Let everything be as it was before!

ANNA. Off you go, my dear, off you go! Married! You do love me don't you? Why bring your wife into it? Go on, quick march! We'll talk later, in an hour or so . . . Now you're in the grip of some seizure of deceit . . .

PLATONOV. I wouldn't know how to deceive you! (*Speaking quietly into her ear.*) If I knew how to deceive you, I would have been your lover long ago . . .

ANNA (*brusquely*). Get out!

PLATONOV. You're lying, you're not really angry! You're only just saying that . . . (*He goes into the house.*)

ANNA. Extraordinary creature! (*She sits down.*) Doesn't realise what he's saying . . . Juggling every kind of love! Just like a man novelist making love to a woman novelist! (*Pause.*) Insufferable fellow! We'll go on chattering till doomsday like this, my dear friend. I haven't taken him fairly, I'll take him by force . . . This very night! High time both of us ended this ridiculous state of expectancy! Tired of it! . . . I'll take him by force . . .

PORFIRI GLAGOLYEV *enters.*

PORFIRI GLAGOLYEV. You're here? (*He sits down beside her.*) I was looking for you Anna Petrovna! There's something I want to discuss with you.

ANNA. Well then, let's discuss . . .

PORFIRI GLAGOLYEV. I'd like to talk over . . . I'd like to know your answer to my . . . letter . . . You know of course that I renounce a husband's rights. What need have I of rights! I need a friend, my house needs an intelligent mistress . . . My house is a paradise, but in it there are no . . . angels.

ANNA. I often ask myself what I'd do in heaven. Forgive me, Porfiri Semyonovich, but I really don't understand your proposal! Why do you want to marry? Why have you set your mind on a friend in a skirt? It's no business of mine, forgive me, but were I your age, had I your money, intelligence and integrity, I'd seek nothing else in this life but the common good . . . how can I put it? I'd seek nothing but to satisfy my love for my neighbour.

PORFIRI GLAGOLYEV. I don't know how to fight for people's happiness! I was born only to admire great deeds and to perform a host of paltry ones that are utterly worthless! Just to admire . . . Won't you come to me?

ANNA. No, don't say another word about it! Don't attach any vital significance to my refusal . . . It's all vanity of vanities, dear friend! What's that noise? I'll wager it's Platonov creating a disturbance! What a character!

GREKOVA *and* NIKOLAI TRILETSKI *enter.*

GREKOVA. It's greater than any other possible insult! (*She weeps.*) Greater! Only depraved creatures could be capable of remaining silent . . .

NIKOLAI TRILETSKI. Yes, yes, but what have I to do with it? I can't take a cudgel to him, can I?

GREKOVA. You're a coward, that's what you are! Leave me! Go to your revolting cold buffet! Good-bye! Spare yourself the trouble of coming to see me any more! We don't need each other!

NIKOLAI TRILETSKI. I'm sick of it all, I find it all infinitely repulsive! Tears, tears . . . God! (*He goes out.*)

ANNA (*going over to her*). Marya Yefimovna! (*Kissing her.*) Don't cry, my dear! Women were created to endure all kinds of nastiness at the hands of men . . .

GREKOVA. Oh, but not me! I'll . . . have him discharged! He has no right to be a schoolmaster! I'll go tomorrow to see the District School Inspector.

ANNA. What did he do to you?

GREKOVA. He kissed me in front of everyone . . . he called me a nincompoop . . . and . . . shoved me on to a table . . . Don't imagine that this will pass unrewarded! Either he's a madman or . . . I'll show him! (*She goes off.*)

ANNA (*calling after her*). Good-bye! A bientôt! (*To* YAKOV.) Get Marya Yefimovna's carriage! Oh, Platonov, Platonov! All his brawling will land him in trouble one day! . . .

PORFIRI GLAGOLYEV. Such a splendid girl! Our dear Mikhail Vasilyevich has taken a dislike to her. He ill-treats her . . .

ANNA. Not a bit of it! Today he insults her and tomorrow he asks her forgiveness! It's the grand seigneur in him!

KIRIL GLAGOLYEV *enters.*

KIRIL GLAGOLYEV (*aside*). He's with her again! Damn disgrace! (*He looks intently at his father.*)

PORFIRI GLAGOLYEV (*after a pause*). What's the matter with you?

KIRIL GLAGOLYEV. Here you sit and they're looking for you back there! Go on then, they're calling you!

PORFIRI GLAGOLYEV. Who's calling me?

KIRIL GLAGOLYEV. People!

PORFIRI GLAGOLYEV. Of course, I know it's people! (*Rising.*) As you please, but I shan't let you alone, Anna Petrovna! When you've understood me, you may have something else to say! See you later . . . (*He goes into the house.*)

KIRIL GLAGOLYEV (*sitting down beside her*). The old badger! The ass! No one's calling him! I just pulled the wool over his eyes!

ANNA. When you grow to be a little more sensible, you'll give yourself a good scolding on your father's behalf!

KIRIL GLAGOLYEV. You're joking! . . . Here's why I came here . . . Just two words: Yes or no?

ANNA. What do you mean?

KIRIL GLAGOLYEV (*laughing*). As though you didn't understand! Yes or no?

ANNA. I certainly don't understand!

KIRIL GLAGOLYEV. You'll understand in a minute! Gold needs no interpreting! If it's yes, would you not care, generalissimus of my heart, to slip your hand into my pocket and pull out of it my wallet with papa's money?

He turns his side pocket towards her.

ANNA. Frankly now . . . Why, intelligent people are slapped in the face for saying such things!

KIRIL GLAGOLYEV. One doesn't mind a slap in the face from a nice lady . . . First she slaps your face and then a little while later she goes on to say 'yes'! . . .

ANNA (*rising*). Take your cap and get out of here this very minute!

KIRIL GLAGOLYEV (*rising*). Where?

ANNA. Wherever you like! Get out of here and don't ever dare show your face here again!

KIRIL GLAGOLYEV. Oh, but why are you so angry? I shan't go, Anna Petrovna!

ANNA. Then I'll order you to be shown out! (*She goes into the house.*)

KIRIL GLAGOLYEV. You're so angry! I didn't say anything in particular! What did I say? There's no need to be angry!

He follows her.

PLATONOV *and* SOFYA *come out of the house.*

PLATONOV. So I still remain at the school in a post for which I am completely unsuited – schoolmaster! That's what happened after we parted! (*They sit down.*) Evil swarms around me, sullies the land, swallows up my compatriots and brothers in Christ; yet here I sit, arms folded, resting! I sit, I look on, I'm silent! . . . I'm twenty-seven, when I'm thirty I'll be exactly the same – I can see no changes in the future! And then? More overfed slovenliness, torpor, a complete indifference to all that is not flesh, and finally death! A life wasted! The hair of my head stands on end when I think of that death! (*Pause.*) How is one to rise again, Sofya Yegorovna? (*Pause.*) You're silent, you don't know . . . And how are you to know? Sofya Yegorovna, I'm not sorry for myself; to hell with it, with this 'me'! But what has happened to you? Where is your purity of soul, your sincerity, your truthfulness, your audacity? (SOFYA *rises.* PLATONOV *makes her sit down.*) Wait! This is my last word! What has turned you into such a posturing, idle phrasemonger? Who taught you to lie? And what kind of a person were you before! How splendid you were, Sofya Yegorovna! Darling Sofya Yegorovna, perhaps it's not too late, perhaps you can still rise up! Think about it! Gather up all your strength and rise up for God's own sake! (*Seizing her by the hand.*) My dearest, tell me frankly, for the sake of our common past, what forced you to marry such a man? What tempted you to such a marriage?

SOFYA. He's an excellent man . . .

PLATONOV. Don't say things you don't believe!

SOFYA (*rising*). He's my husband, I must ask you . . .

PLATONOV. Let him be whatever he likes, I'll speak the truth! Sit down! (*Making her sit down.*) Why didn't you choose someone who works, who suffers? Why didn't you take someone else and not this pigmy besmirched with debts and sloth? . . .

SOFYA (*rising and burying her face in her hands*). Leave me alone! (*A noise is heard from the house.*) Get away! (*She goes towards the house.*)

PLATONOV (*following her*). You won't leave, will you? Of course not! Let's be friends, Sophie! You're not going away? Shall we have another talk? Yes? (*A still louder noise from the house. One can hear the sound of people running up and down the stairs.*)

SOFYA. Yes.

PLATONOV. Let's be friends, my dear . . . Why should we be enemies? Look . . . Just a word or two more . . .

VOINITSEV *runs out of the house followed by guests.*

VOINITSEV. Ah, here they are, the most important ones of all! Come on, let's set the fireworks off! (*Shouting.*) Yakov, quick march to the river! (*To* SOFYA.) Have you changed your mind, Sophie?

PLATONOV. She won't leave, she's staying . . .

VOINITSEV. Yes? In that case – hurrah! Your hand, Mikhail Vasilyevich! (*He shakes his hand.*) I always did believe in your eloquence! Let's go and set the fireworks off! (*He goes off with the guests into the garden.*)

PLATONOV (*after a pause*). Yes, that's how it is, Sofya Yegorovna! . . . Hm . . .

VOINITSEV (*offstage*). Maman, where are you? Platonov!

A pause.

PLATONOV. To hell with it, I'll go too . . . (*Shouting.*) Sergei

Pavlovich, wait! Wait for me! Send Yakov here to fetch the balloon. (*He runs into the garden.*)

ANNA (*running out of the house*). Wait, everyone! Sergei, wait! They're not all here yet! Go on firing the cannon until we're ready! (*To* SOFYA.) Go on, Sophie! Why are you looking so crestfallen?

PLATONOV (*offstage*). This way, milady! We'll strike up the old song! Never mind the new ones!

ANNA. Coming, mon cher! (*She runs off.*)

SOFYA. To go or not to go? (*She is plunged in thought.*)

NIKOLAI TRILETSKI (*entering*). Hey, where are you? (*Singing.*) Coming, coming! (*He stops and looks* SOFYA *in the eye.*)

SOFYA. What do you want?

NIKOLAI TRILETSKI. Nothing . . .

SOFYA. Well then, get away with you! I'm not in the mood either for talking or listening . . .

NIKOLAI TRILETSKI. I know, I know . . . (*Pause.*) For some reason or other I feel terribly like passing my finger over your forehead: what is it made of, your forehead? I feel terribly like doing it! Not to insult you, but just . . . you know . . . for the sake of continence . . .

SOFYA. Buffoon! (*She turns away.*) Not just a comedian, a buffoon, a clown!

NIKOLAI TRILETSKI. Yes . . . a buffoon! It's for my buffoonery that I get my grub from the general's lady . . . yes . . . and my pocket-money. It's true, what I say, isn't it? Anyway, I'm not the only one to say it . . . You said it too when you were staying at Glagolyev's . . .

SOFYA. Good, good! I'm very glad they passed it on to you! So now you know that I can distinguish between buffoons and wits! If you were an actor, you'd be the favourite of the gods, but the stalls would hiss at you. I hiss at you!

NIKOLAI TRILETSKI. A supernaturally successful witticism! Most commendable! I beg to take my leave. (*He bows.*) Till our next pleasant meeting! I'd like to go on talking to you, but . . . I quail . . . I am routed! (*He goes off into the garden.*)

SOFYA (*stamping her foot*). Good-for-nothing! He doesn't really know my opinion of him! Futile little man!

PLATONOV (*offstage*). Who's coming out on to the river with me?

SOFYA. What's to be, can't be escaped! (*Shouting.*) Coming! (*She runs off.* PORFIRI *and* KIRIL GLAGOLYEV *come out of the house.*)

PORFIRI GLAGOLYEV. You're lying! You're lying, you disgusting urchin!

KIRIL GLAGOLYEV. What nonsense! Why on earth should I lie? Ask her yourself if you don't believe me! The moment you left, I whispered a few words in her ear, gave her a hug, then a nice, big, juicy kiss . . . First she asked for three thousand, but I bargained with her and beat her down to one thousand. So now give me one thousand roubles!

PORFIRI GLAGOLYEV. Kiril, it's the honour of a woman you're talking about! Don't besmirch it! It's sacred!

KIRIL GLAGOLYEV. But . . . I embraced her, I tell you! What's so surprising about that? All women are like that nowadays! Don't you believe their innocence! I know them! And you want to get married, too! (*He laughs.*)

PORFIRI GLAGOLYEV. For God's sake, Kiril, don't you know what slander is?

KIRIL GLAGOLYEV. Give me one thousand roubles! I'll hand them over to her in your presence! He doesn't believe that I can conquer women! Offer her two thousand and she's yours! I know women, old chap!

PORFIRI GLAGOLYEV (*taking his wallet out of his pocket and throwing it down*). Take it.

KIRIL GLAGOLYEV *picks up the wallet and counts the money.*

VOINITSEV (*offstage*). I'm starting! Maman, fire! Triletski, climb up on to the summer-house! Who's stepped on to the box? You!

NIKOLAI TRILETSKI (*offstage*). I'm climbing! Hell? (*Laughing.*) Who's that? I've stepped on to Bugrov's head! Where are the matches?

KIRIL GLAGOLYEV (*aside*). I'm revenged! (*Shouting.*) Hurra-a-ah! (*He runs off.*)

NIKOLAI TRILETSKI (*offstage*). Who's that shouting there? Give it to him in the neck!

VOINITSEV (*offstage*). Shall we begin?

PORFIRI GLAGOLYEV (*clutching his head*). Oh, my God, the depravity! Filth! I worshipped her! Lord forgive her! (*He sits down on a bench and buries his face in his hands.*)

VOINITSEV (*offstage*). Who's taken the string? Maman, aren't you ashamed of yourself? Where's my string that was lying here?

ANNA (*offstage*). Here it is, you gaper!

PORFIRI GLAGOLYEV *falls from the bench.*

ANNA (*offstage*). You! Who is it? Don't tramp about here! (*Shouting.*) Give it here! Give it here! (SOFYA *runs in.*)

SOFYA (*pale, her hair ruffled*). I can't! It's too much, I haven't the strength to resist! (*She clutches her bosom.*) My doom . . . or . . . happiness! I can't breathe here! . . . Either he'll destroy me or . . . he's the harbinger of a new life! I welcome you, I bless you, you, my new life! It's decided!

VOINITSEV (*offstage, shouting*). Look out! (*The firework display begins.*)

Curtain

SCENE TWO

A cutting in the forest. At the beginning of the cutting, to the left – a schoolhouse. Along the cutting, losing itself in the distance, stretches a railway track, which, near the schoolhouse, takes a turn to the right. There is a row of telegraph poles. It is night.

SASHA *is sitting at an open window and* OSIP, *with a rifle slung over his shoulder, is standing in front of the window.*

OSIP. How did it happen? Very simply. I was walking along a forest path not far from here, and there she was: she'd tucked up her dress and was scooping up water out of the stream. She'd scoop, then she'd drink, she'd scoop, then she'd drink, and then wet her head . . . I climbed down and came up close, staring at her all the time. And she went on, paying no attention to me, just as if she were saying: you fool, you're only a peasant, so why should I take any notice of you? 'Milady,' I says, 'Your Excellency felt like having a nice, cool drink of water, I suppose?' 'And what business is it of yours?' she says. 'Go on, get back to where you came from!' She says this and doesn't even look at me . . . I began to feel shy . . . I even began to feel ashamed, I felt hurt that I was of peasant stock . . . 'Why are you looking at me, booby?' she says. 'Haven't you ever seen a human being before, or what?' And she gave me a piercing look . . . 'Or perhaps,' she says, 'perhaps you've taken a fancy to me?' 'I have taken a terrible fancy to you,' I says. 'You're so noble-looking, Your Excellency, so beautiful . . . I've never in all my days,' I says, 'I've never seen anyone so beautiful! Beside you our village beauty Masha is a horse, a camel! I think if I was to kiss you,' I says, 'I'd die on this very spot!' She burst out laughing . . . 'Well then, go on,' she says. 'Kiss me, if you want to!' The moment she said this, I felt a fever come on all over me. I went up to her, took her gently by the shoulder and kissed her as hard as I could right here, in this very spot, cheek and neck at the same time . . .

SASHA (*laughing*). And what did she do?

OSIP. 'And now,' she says, 'make yourself scarce! And wash yourself more often,' she says, 'and don't neglect your fingernails!' And so I moved off.

SASHA. How bold she is! (*She gives* OSIP *a plate of cabbage soup.*) There, eat that! Sit down somewhere! Take your cap off! It's sinful to eat with your cap on. And say your Grace too!

OSIP (*taking off his cap*). I haven't gone in for any piety for a long time now . . . (*He eats.*) And since that time I've gone clean off my head as it were . . . Would you believe it? I don't eat, I don't sleep . . . I've got her in front of my eyes all the time . . . Sometimes I close my eyes and there she is in front of me! I nearly went and drowned myself . . . I even thought of shooting her husband, the general . . . And when she became a widow, I began to run all kinds of messages for her . . . I shot partridge for her, caught quail, painted her summer-house all different colours . . . Once I brought her a live wolf! Whatever she ordered, I'd do it . . . If she'd order me to gobble myself up, I'd gobble myself up! Tender feelings! There's nothing one can do about them!

SASHA. Yes . . . When I fell in love with Mikhail Vasilyevich, before I knew that he loved me too, I was terribly miserable. Sinful woman! Several times I even prayed God to let me die . . .

OSIP. There, do you see? That's what feelings are like! (*He drinks what is left straight out of the plate.*) You wouldn't be having any more soup, would you? (*He hands her the plate.*)

SASHA (*disappears and after half a minute reappears at the window with a small saucepan*). There's no more cabbage soup, but here, would you like some potatoes? They're fried in goose dripping . . .

OSIP. Merci . . . (*He takes the saucepan and eats.*) And so it went on and on. Last year after Easter I brought her a hare. 'Here you are, Your Excellency,' I says, 'here's a little cross-eyed beastie I've brought you.' She takes it into her hands, strokes it and asks me: 'Is it true, what they say,

Osip, that you are a brigand?' 'Yes, it's gospel truth,' I says. 'People wouldn't go round saying that kind of thing for nothing.' So I went and told her everything. 'We must reform you,' she says. 'Off you go,' she says, 'on foot to Kiev. From Kiev go to Moscow, from Moscow to the Trinity Monastery, from there to the New Jerusalem Monastery and then come home. Go on this pilgrimage and in a year's time, you'll be a different man.' So I made myself look like a beggar, took my satchel and set off for Kiev . . . But it didn't work out right! . . . Wonderful spuds! Near Kharkov I fell in with a fine little gang, drank away all my money, got into a brawl and came back home. I even lost my passport. (*Pause.*) Now she won't take anything from me . . . She's angry with me!

SASHA. Why don't you go to church, Osip?

OSIP. I'd go, but you know . . . People will start laughing . . . See, they'll say, he's come to repent! I'm even afraid to walk near the church by day . . . Lot of people about; they might kill me.

SASHA. Well then, why do you go about harming poor folks?

OSIP. And why shouldn't I harm them? It's something you wouldn't understand, Alexandra Ivanovna! A woman like you wouldn't know about such things. And what about Mikhail Vasilyevich? Doesn't he ever harm anyone?

SASHA. Never. If ever he does harm anyone, it's accidental. It's never on purpose. He's a kind man!

OSIP (*handing back the saucepan*). Thanks! (*He sighs.*) You're a fine woman, Alexandra Ivanovna! You haven't got even a drop of woman's malice in you, have you, Alexandra Ivanovna? Pious and godly! (*Laughing.*) It's the first time I've ever seen such woman! Saint Alexandra, pray for us sinners! (*He bows.*) All hail, Saint Alexandra!

SASHA. I can hear Mikhail Vasilyevich coming!

OSIP. You're having me on . . . Right now he's having a heart-to-heart talk with the young lady . . . He's a handsome man! If he wanted to, he could have the whole of the female sex after him! He's got the gift of the gab, he has . . . (*He laughs.*) He makes up to the general's lady all the time . . . Well, that one will tweak his nose for him, she won't give a hang about his being handsome! Reckon he'd be willing, but she . . .

SASHA. That's silly chatter now . . . I don't like it . . . Go, and God be with you . . .

OSIP. I'll go in a minute . . . You should have been in bed a long time ago . . . Waiting up for your husband, I suppose?

SASHA. Yes . . .

OSIP. A good wife! Platonov must have spent a good ten years looking round for such wife; he must have offered up a lot of candles to the saints . . . And in the end, somehow he managed to find one . . . (*He bows.*) Well, good-bye, Alexandra Ivanovna. Good night!

SASHA (*yawning*). Go, and God be with you!

OSIP. I'm going. (*He moves off.*) I'm going off home . . . In my home I've got the earth for a floor, the sky for a ceiling, but where the walls and the roof are no one knows. It's the house you live in if God's curse is on you! It's a big house, but there's nowhere to lay one's head . . . The only good thing about it is that you don't have to pay rates! (*Stopping.*) Good night, Alexandra Ivanovna! Come and see me sometime! In the forest! Just ask for Osip, every bird and squirrel will know! Just look how that stump is shining! Just like a dead man getting out of his grave! My mother used to tell me that if a tree stump shines in the night, it's because there's a sinner buried underneath, and the stump shines so that people will pray for him . . . There'll be a stump shining above my head too . . . I'm just another sinner . . . (*He goes off; after about two minutes he is heard whistling.*)

SASHA (*coming out of the schoolhouse with a candle and a book*). A long time Misha's taking to get home! (*She sits.*) Where did I get to? Misha said I had to read this, so I must read it . . . (*She yawns and reads.*) 'It's high time that we proclaimed once more those great, eternal ideals of mankind, those immortal principles of freedom which were the guiding stars of our fathers and which we, unfortunately, have betrayed.' . . . What does that mean? (*She thinks.*) Don't understand it . . . Why don't they write so that everyone can understand? I'll leave out the Preface . . . 'Masoch' . . . What a funny name . . . Must be foreign . . . 'On a cheerful winter's evening . . .' (*She yawns.*) Oh, I can skip that . . . It's only description . . . (*She turns over a number of pages.*) 'It was difficult to make out who was playing and on what instrument . . . The powerful, majestic sounds of an organ played by an iron masculine hand alternated with the tender sounds of a flute, as if pressed to lovely, feminine lips . . . and finally died away . . .' Tsss . . . Someone's coming! (*Pause.*) It's Misha's footsteps . . . (*She puts out the candle.*) At last . . . (*She gets up and shouts.*) Oo-oo! One, two, one, two! Left, right, left, right! Left, left!

PLATONOV *enters.*

PLATONOV (*entering*). Just to spite you: right, right!

SASHA. Come here, my little sot! Come and sit here! (*She throws her arms around his neck.*)

PLATONOV (*sitting down*). And why aren't you in bed, you infusorian, you?

SASHA. Don't feel like sleep. (*She sits beside him.*) They have kept you late!

PLATONOV (*sitting down*). Yes, they have. Has the express gone through yet?

SASHA. Not yet. The goods train passed through about an hour ago.

PLATONOV. So it's not two yet. Been back a long time?

SASHA. I was back here by ten.

PLATONOV. By the way . . . Did it happen while you were there? Old Glagolyev had a stroke!

SASHA. No!

PLATONOV. Yes . . . Your brother let his blood and sang 'requiescat in pace' . . .

SASHA. I can imagine how scared Anna Petrovna and Sofya Yegorovna were! What a nice person Sofya Yegorovna is! I don't often see such pretty little ladies . . . There's something really special about her . . . (*Pause.*)

PLATONOV. U-ugh! Stupid, vile . . .

SASHA. What?

PLATONOV. What have I done? (*Burying his face in his hands.*) Shame on me!

SASHA. What have you done?

PLATONOV. When have I ever done anything that I've not been ashamed of afterwards?

SASHA (*aside*). He's drunk, the poor boy! (*To him.*) Let's go to bed!

PLATONOV. I was disgusting as never before! Go on, respect yourself after a thing like that! There's no greater misfortune than to be deprived of one's own self-respect! My God! There's nothing positive in me at all, nothing deserving respect or love! (*Pause.*) Now you here, you love me . . . I don't understand it! So you've found something in me that you can love? Do you love me?

SASHA. What a question! How could I not love you?

PLATONOV. I know, but name me that good thing for which you love me so much! Show me that good thing you love in me!

SASHA. Hm . . . What do I love you for? What a funny creature you are, Misha! How can I not love you if you're my husband?

PLATONOV. So you only love me for being your husband?

SASHA. I don't understand you.

PLATONOV. You don't understand? (*Laughing.*) Oh, you're

my little fathead, you are! Why weren't you a little fly? With your brains, you'd be the wisest little fly that ever was! (*He kisses her brow.*) What would happen to you if you understood me? Don't try to understand, my treasure, don't seek to know, if you want to go on loving me! (*He kisses her hand.*) My little doe! By the grace of your ignorance I too am happy! I have a family like everybody else . . . I have a family . . . (SASHA *laughs.*) My treasure! Darling, silly, little peasant wench! You're no ordinary, live wife; I ought to be keeping you on a table, under a glass bell! And how did we contrive, you and I, to bring little Nikolai into this world? You shouldn't be having babies, you should be making little ginger-bread men . . .

SASHA. What nonsense you're talking, Misha!

PLATONOV. Heaven forbid that you should understand! After all, the earth is supported on the backs of whales, and the whales are propped up by pitchforks . . . Eh? (*He laughs.*) Where would we get faithful and constant wives if it weren't for women like you, Sasha? (*He tries to kiss her.*)

SASHA (*not letting him*). Get away! (*Angrily.*) And why did you marry me if I'm so stupid? Should have got yourself a clever one! I didn't stop you!

PLATONOV (*laughing*). And you know how to lose your temper too! But this is a revelation! You're capable of anger too? You're not joking?

SASHA (*rising*). Off to bed with you, chum! You always get revelations when you've had too much to drink! Drunkard! And he's a teacher, what's more! You're not a teacher, you're just a pig-face! Go to bed! (*She smacks him on the back and goes into the schoolhouse.*)

PLATONOV (*alone*). Am I really drunk? I can't be, I didn't drink much . . . But there's something strange going on in my head . . . (*Pause.*) And when I was talking to Sofya, was I . . . drunk? (*He thinks.*) No, I wasn't! I wasn't, more's the pity! I wasn't! (*He jumps up.*) What wrong has her unfortunate husband done me? Why should I go and smear him with such filth in her eyes? My conscience will never forgive me this! I let my tongue run away with itself, I posed, I strutted, I boasted . . . She listened to a fool's ravings with eyes downcast! She went all limp and soft, the poor wretch! Absurd! Repulsive! I'm a scoundrel! A comical scoundrel! An extremely unusual scoundrel! . . . (*Pause.*) I must get away . . . I'll ask the inspector to give me another post . . . I'll write off to him this very day . . .

ISAK VENGEROVICH *enters.*

ISAK VENGEROVICH. Hm. Not sleeping and not scolding anyone! . . . He's not in his normal state! (*To* PLATONOV.) Not gone to bed yet?

PLATONOV. As you see. But why have you stopped here? Permit me to bid you a good night!

ISAK VENGEROVICH. I'll go in a minute. You give yourself up to solitude? (*Looking around.*) You feel yourself lord of all nature? On such a delightful night . . . May one sit next to you?

PLATONOV. You may.

ISAK VENGEROVICH. Thank you. (*He sits down.*) I like to say thank you for everything. Where is your lady friend, Platonov? Why, all these sounds, all this murmuring of nature, this singing and chirping of crickets only lack the whispers of love – and you're in paradise! With this coquettish, timid breeze, all you need is the hot breath of a dear one to make your cheeks blaze with happiness! The murmurings of Mother Nature lack words of love . . . Woman! You look at me with amazement. Ha-ha! I have begun to talk a language that is not my own? You're right . . . It's not my language. When I'm sober, I shall blush for what I've said . . . Anyway, why shouldn't I indulge in a little poetic chatter? Who will stop me?

PLATONOV. No one.

ISAK VENGEROVICH. Or, perhaps, this language of the gods does not accord with my position? My face isn't poetic?

PLATONOV. It isn't poetic.

ISAK VENGEROVICH. It isn't poetic . . . Hm . . . No Jew's physiognomy is poetic. It was just nature's little joke: she didn't give us Jews poetic physiognomies! . . . They say that the Jews have no poets . . .

PLATONOV. Who says it?

ISAK VENGEROVICH. Everybody says it, and yet how many real poets we have, not like Pushkin or Lermontov, but real ones: Heine, Goethe . . .

PLATONOV. Goethe was a German.

ISAK VENGEROVICH. A Jew!

PLATONOV. A German!

ISAK VENGEROVICH. A Jew! I know what I'm talking about!

PLATONOV. And I know what I'm talking about, but have it your way! There's no arguing with a half-educated Jew!

ISAK VENGEROVICH. No there isn't . . . (*Pause.*) And even if we hadn't any poets, all the better! A poet is usually a sponger, an egoist . . . Did Goethe ever give a piece of bread to a single German proletarian?

PLATONOV. An old tune! Enough, young man! He never took a piece of bread from a German proletarian! That is what matters . . . And then, it's better to be a poet than to be nothing . . . a billion times better! (*Pause.*)

ISAK VENGEROVICH. Just look at the sky! Yes . . . It's good here, peaceful; there are only trees here . . . Yes, but it's not for me the trees are murmuring . . . And the moon doesn't look down on me as kindly as on this Platonov here . . . It's as though she were saying 'you're not one of us – get away from here, get back to your nasty little Yiddish shop!' However, that's nonsense . . . Anyway, personal happiness is only egoism!

PLATONOV (*who has been examining* VENGEROVICH'S *gold watch chain*). A fine chain you've got there! What seals! And how it shines!

ISAK VENGEROVICH. So you're taken with my chain? (*He laughs.*) Does this tinsel lure you? Take it then! (*He throws the chain down on the ground.*) How lucky you are that you don't have to experience all the weight of this filthy gold! My fetters of gold!

PLATONOV. The fetters aren't always secure! Our fathers dissolved them in drink.

ISAK VENGEROVICH. How many there are that are unhappy, that are hungry beneath this moon! When at last will the millions that sow much and reap nothing cease to go hungry? When, I ask you? Platonov, why don't you reply?

PLATONOV. Leave me! I don't like bells that go on ringing incessantly and to no purpose! Forgive me, but leave me alone! I want to sleep!

ISAK VENGEROVICH. I'm a bell? Hm . . . You, rather, are the bell . . .

PLATONOV. I'm a bell and you're a bell; the only difference is that I ring myself, whereas you are rung by others . . . Good night! (*He rises.*)

ISAK VENGEROVICH. Good night! (*A clock inside the school strikes two.*) Already two . . . I don't offer you my hand and I'm proud of it! You haven't the right to shake my hand . . .

PLATONOV. What nonsense! It's all one to me . . . (ISAK VENGEROVICH *goes upstage, then returns.*) What do you want?

ISAK VENGEROVICH. I left my chain here somewhere . . .

PLATONOV. Here it is, your chain! (*He kicks the chain over to him.*) So you didn't forget it after all! Listen, be generous, give up this chain to help an acquaintance of mine who can be classified as one of those that sow much and eat nothing! This chain will feed him and his family for years on end! Will you permit me to pass it on to him?

ISAK VENGEROVICH. No . . . I'd give it away with pleasure,

but, on my word of honour, I can't! It's a present, a keepsake . . .

PLATONOV. Yes, yes . . . Clear off!

ISAK VENGEROVICH (*picks up the chain*). Leave me alone, please! (*With an air of exhaustion goes upstage, sits on the railway track and buries his face in his hands.*)

PLATONOV. The vulgarity of it! To be young and at the same time not to have a pure soul! What profound depravity! (*He sits.*) And to think that once I resembled this . . . Oh!

Horse's hooves are heard. ANNA PETROVNA *enters in riding habit carrying a hunting crop.*

PLATONOV. Madame la générale!

ANNA. I knew you wouldn't be asleep yet! And how can one sleep now? God gave us the winter to sleep in! Good evening, man meat! (*Offering her hand.*) Well? What's the matter with you? Your hand! (PLATONOV *offers his hand.*) You're not drunk, are you?

PLATONOV. God knows! Either I'm sober, or I'm as drunk as the most inveterate drunkard . . . And what are you up to? Riding off your fat, my dear somnambulist?

ANNA (*sitting down beside him*). M-yes . . . (*Pause.*) Yes, my dear Mikhail Vasilyevich. (*She hums for a moment, then laughs.*) What big, wondering eyes! (*Pause.*)

PLATONOV. So I see you've taken it into your head to spend your time playing the goat . . .

ANNA. In my old age . . .

PLATONOV. One could forgive old women in their dotage . . . But you . . . You're as young as the summer in June. Your life is in front of you.

ANNA. I want my life here and now, not somewhere in front of me . . . And I am young, Platonov, it's terrible how young I am! I feel it! This youth keeps on blowing all over me like a breeze! Damn young . . . (*She shivers.*) Damn cold!

Pause.

PLATONOV (*jumping up*). I beg of you! Hm . . . Why do you look at me like that? But just . . . just think!

ANNA. I've already thought . . .

PLATONOV. Just you think, you proud, intelligent, splendid woman! Such intelligence, such beauty and youth . . . and you come to me! I can't believe my eyes or my ears . . . She's come to conquer, to storm the fortress! I'm no fortress! There's nothing for you to conquer here . . . I – am weakness, terrible weakness! Understand that, can't you!

ANNA (*rising and coming up to him*). Self-abasement mightier than pride . . . How is it to be then, Michel? Somehow we must resolve this. Agree yourself that . . .

PLATONOV. I'm not going to resolve it, since I never started it!

ANNA. Ugh . . . a nasty philosophy! And aren't you ashamed to lie? On such a night, under such a sky . . . and you're prepared to tell lies? Tell your lies in autumn, if you want to, when there's mud and slush, but not now, not here . . . They can hear you, they're watching you . . . Just take a look up there, you ridiculous fellow! (*Pause.*) Even the stars are twinkling up there to say that you're lying . . . Enough, dear fellow! Be good, as all this is good! Don't violate this calm with your petty little self . . . Drive your demons away from you. (*Putting one arm around him.*) There is no other man that I could love as I love you. There is no woman that you could love as you love me . . . Let us take for ourselves just this love . . . (*She kisses him.*)

PLATONOV. Odysseus was worthy of having the sirens sing to him, but I'm not King Odysseus, siren! (*He embraces her.*) If only I could make you happy! How lovely you are! But I shan't make you happy! I'll make you what I've made all the women that have thrown themselves at me . . . I'll make you unhappy!

ANNA. You think so much about yourself! Are you really so awful, Don Juan? (*She laughs.*) But how pretty you are in the moonlight! Lovely! (*They sit down on the railway track.*)

PLATONOV. If I were an honourable man, I'd leave you . . . I had a premonition of this today . . . I'm a scoundrel! Why didn't I leave then?

ANNA. Drive your demons away from you, Michel! Don't poison yourself . . . Why, it's a woman that's come to you, not a wild beast . . . All right, I'll go away if you want me to! Do you want me to? I'll go and everything will be as it was before! . . . All right? (*She laughs.*) Booby! Take, seize, grab! . . . What more do you want? Smoke me to the end, like a cigarette, wring me till I'm dry, cut me up into little pieces . . . Be a man! (*She shakes him.*) Funny boy!

PLATONOV. But were you really intended for me? (*He kisses her hands.*) Go to another, my darling . . . Go to one that's worthy of you . . .

ANNA. Oh . . . Will you stop talking drivel! Look, it's very simple: a woman comes to you, she loves you, you love her . . . The weather is delightful . . . What could be simpler? So what's the point of all this political philosophy? Are you posing for a pretty picture, or what?

PLATONOV. Hm . . . (*He stands up.*) And if you've come just to play the fool with me, just to have a little debauchery? . . . Then what? You know, don't you, that I'm not for temporary use . . . I won't allow myself to be played with! You won't pension me off with a few coppers as you have a dozen others! . . . I cost far too much for some paltry little intrigue . . . (*He seizes his head in his hands.*) To respect, to love you and at the same time . . . the plebeian vulgarity of it, the bourgeois pettiness! . . .

ANNA (*coming up to him*). You love me, you respect me, so why are you haggling with me? Why say all these disgusting things to me? Why all these 'ifs'? I love you . . . I've told you myself and you yourself know that I love you . . . What more do you want? I want to rest . . . (*She rests her head on his chest.*) Rest . . . Don't you understand that, Platonov? I want to rest . . . I want oblivion and nothing else . . . You don't know . . . you don't know how difficult life is for me, and I . . . want to live!

PLATONOV (*seizing her by the hand*). Listen! . . . For the last time! . . . I'm speaking to you as an honest man . . . Leave! For the last time! Leave!

ANNA (*laughing*). Are you joking? You're making a fool of yourself, you know! I shan't leave you, not now! (*She throws her arms round his neck.*) Do you hear? For the last time I tell you: I won't let you go! Come what may, no matter what happens! Destroy me, perish yourself, still I'll take you! Live! Tra-ta-ta-ta . . . ra-ra-ra . . . You're mine! . . .

PLATONOV. Once more . . . As an honest man . . .

ANNA. I haven't taken him fairly, I'll take him by force . . . If you love me, go on and love me and stop playing silly rabbits! Tra-t-ta-ta-ta . . . (*She sings.*) 'Peal of victory ring forth! . . .' Hurrah, hurrah! (*She throws a black scarf over his head.*) Hurrah!

PLATONOV (*laughing*). Empty-headed woman! You're asking for trouble! . . . You'll weep, you know! I won't allow myself to be trifled with . . . We'll see who's going to do the trifling . . . and with whom! . . . Well, shall we go?

ANNA (*laughing*). Allons! (*She takes him by the arm.*) Wait . . . Someone's coming . . . Here! (*They hide behind a tree.*) Why don't you write leaders for newspapers? I'm not joking . . .

NIKOLAI TRILETSKI *enters.*

NIKOLAI TRILETSKI (*goes up to the schoolhouse and knocks at the window*). Sasha! Sister! Sasha, my pet!

SASHA (*opening the window*). Who's there? Is it you, Nikolai? What do you want?

NIKOLAI TRILETSKI. Aren't you in bed yet? Let me stay the night, sweetie!

SASHA. If you like . . .

NIKOLAI TRILETSKI. You can put me in the class-room . . . My head's spinning awfully . . . I see everything double . . . I'm standing in front of one window and it seems to me that there are two of them: which one am I going to climb in through? A good thing I'm not married, otherwise I'd think I was a bigamist . . . Everything's double! You've got two heads, one on each neck! By the way . . . I was blowing my nose over by the oak tree that they've chopped down, the one over by the stream, and I must have dropped forty roubles that I had out of my handkerchief . . . Go and find them nice and early in the morning, my pet . . . you can keep them.

SASHA. Oh, what a sloven you are, Nikolai! Oh yes, I nearly forgot . . . The shop-keeper's wife called. You're to go over and see them as quickly as possible . . . Her husband's been taken ill . . . He's had some kind of stroke in his head . . . You'd better go quickly!

NIKOLAI TRILETSKI. Well, the Lord keep him! I'm not up to it . . . I've got shooting pains myself, in my head and in my belly . . . (*He climbs in through the window.*) Move aside . . .

SASHA. Climb in quickly then! You're standing on my dress . . . (*She closes the window.*)

PLATONOV. What the hell! Here's someone else!

ANNA. Wait!

PLATONOV. Don't hold me back . . . I'll go if I want to! Who is it?

ANNA. Petrin and Shcherbuk.

PETRIN *and* SHCHERBUK *enter, swaying about and without their frock-coats. The former wears a black top-hat, the latter a grey one.*

PETRIN. Vivat Petrin, doctor of law! Hurrah! Where's the road? Where have we strayed to? What? What? (*He laughs.*) Here's the Department of National Education, Pavochka! Here's where they teach the bumkins to forget God and to swindle! So that's where we've strayed to . . . Hm . . . So . . . This, brother, is where that . . . Hell, what's his name? . . . Platóshka lives . . . a civilised man . . . Pava, where is Platóshka now, eh? Say what you think, don't be ashamed! Singing a duet with the general's widow, eh? (*He shouts.*) Glagolyev's a fool! She tweaked his nose for him and he went and had a stroke!

SHCHERBUK. I want to go home, Gerasya . . . I'm terribly sleepy! . . . Deuce take the lot of them!

PETRIN (*sighing*). Pava, Pavochka, did you drink 'champagne'? (*He gives the French pronunciation.*) And so I suppose you're drunk now? And whose 'champagne' were you drinking? You were drinking my 'champagne'! . . . Back there what you were drinking was mine and what you were eating was mine . . . The dress the general's widow was wearing is mine, the stockings young Sergei's wearing are mine . . . It's all mine! I've given them everything! And the heels on my own boots are all worn away, they're quite crooked! I've squandered all I have on them and what have I received in return? Go on, ask me, what have I received in return? (*He makes the 'fig' sign.*) Yes! Their lackey misses me out when he's serving dinner and always tries to poke me with his elbow . . . She treats me as if I were some kind of pig . . . The Yid gets more respect . . . The Yid is at the head of the bed and we're at the foot . . . And why? Because the Yid gives more money . . . And on his brow are the fateful words: for sale by public auction! . . . Very good then! Not a copeck more! Do you hear? Not a copeck! I'm going to claim on the bills! Tomorrow! I'll put her in the dirt head first, the ungrateful creature!

SHCHERBUK. She's a count, a baron! She's got the face of a general! Me . . . I'm just a Kalmuk, that's all . . . What an uneven road! There should be a highway with all these telegraph poles . . . with bells . . . ding, ding, ding . . .

They go off.

ANNA (*coming out from behind the tree*). Have they gone?

PLATONOV. They've gone . . .

ANNA (*taking him by the shoulders*). Shall we go on our way?

PLATONOV. Yes. I'm coming, but if only you knew how much I didn't want to! It's not me coming to you, but the devil inside me that keeps on beating me on the head with his: Go, go! God, how I would have thrown you aside if it weren't for this weak, oafish body of mine . . .

ANNA. What filth! (*She strikes him with her hunting crop.*) Talk as much as you like, but mind your language! (*She moves away from him.*) Come if you want to! If you don't I don't give a damn! I'm not going to beg you on my bended knees! It's too much!

PLATONOV. Hey . . . It's too late to take offence! (*He follows her and takes her by the arm; she tears her arm away.*) I'll come . . . You can't stop the demon inside me now! . . . It's only that . . .

SASHA (*appearing at the window*). Misha, Misha! Where are you?

PLATONOV. Hell!

SASHA. Ah . . . I see you . . . Who's that you're with? (*Laughing.*) Anna Petrovna! I scarcely recognised you! You look so black! What is it you're wearing? Hello!

ANNA. Hello, Alexandra Ivanovna!

SASHA. You're in your riding habit? So you're out riding? Excellent idea! Such a fine night! Let's go too, Misha!

ANNA. I've had enough for one night, Alexandra Ivanovna. I'm on my way home . . .

SASHA. In that case, of course . . . Misha, do come in! I really don't know what to do! Kólya's sick . . .

PLATONOV. Which Kólya?

SASHA. Brother Nikolai . . . He must have had a lot to drink . . . Do come in, please! And you come in too, Anna

Petrovna! I'll run down to the cellar and bring up some cream . . . We'll have a glass each . . . Nice, cool cream!

ANNA. Thank you . . . I'm going home now . . . (*To* PLATONOV.) You go in . . . I'll wait for you . . .

SASHA. I can run down to the cellar if you like . . . Come on, Misha . . . (*She disappears.*)

PLATONOV. I'd completely forgotten about her existence. She believes, how she believes! Go . . . I'll put her to bed and then come . . .

ANNA. But be quick . . .

PLATONOV. We very nearly ran into trouble! Good-bye for the present! (*He goes into the schoolhouse.*)

ANNA. I too had completely forgotten she existed . . . (*Pause.*) It's cruel . . . However, it isn't the first time he's had to bamboozle the poor girl! (*She sighs.*) If one's going to sin, one might as well do it properly! God alone will know! Not the first time . . . Damnation! Now wait while he puts her to bed! It'll drag on for an hour, if not more . . .

ISAK VENGEROVICH (*coming up to her*). Anna Petrovna . . . (*He falls on his knees before her.*) Anna Petrovna . . . (*He seizes her by the hand.*) Anna!

ANNA. Who is it? Who are you? (*Bending down towards him.*) Who is it? You, Isak Abramovich? Is it you? What's the matter with you?

ISAK VENGEROVICH. Anna! (*He kisses her hand.*)

ANNA. Go away! It's not right! You are a man!

ISAK VENGEROVICH. Anna!

ANNA. Stop clawing at me! Go away! (*She shoves at his shoulder.*)

ISAK VENGEROVICH (*lying stretched out on the ground*). Oh, it's stupid . . . Stupid! (*He rises.*) Wild, savage, shameful night! (*He creeps off.*)

OSIP (*coming out*). It wouldn't be you by any chance, would it, Your Excellency? (*He bows.*) How did you come to find yourself in this sacred retreat of ours?

ANNA. Is that you, Osip? Hello! Are you spying on me? Espionage? (*She takes him by the chin.*) Did you see everything?

OSIP. Everything.

ANNA. And why are you so pale? Eh? (*She laughs.*) Are you in love with me, Osip?

OSIP. It's just as you like . . .

ANNA. Are you in love?

OSIP. I don't understand you . . . (*He weeps.*) I worshipped you as a saint . . . If you'd ordered me to go through fire, I'd have gone through fire . . .

ANNA. That'll do, booby . . . You can bring me some more little hares . . . I'll accept them again . . . Well, good-bye . . . Come to me tomorrow and I'll give you some money: you'll go to Kiev by train . . . All right? Good-bye . . . And don't you dare touch Platonov, do you hear?

OSIP. From now on I'm not taking any more orders from you . . .

ANNA. Well, how do you like that? Would you have me enter a nunnery perhaps? As though it's his affair! There, there! He's crying! Are you a child or what? That'll do . . . When he sets off to come to me, fire a shot into the air. A good, loud shot. Will you?

OSIP. Yes, I will.

ANNA. That's a good boy . . .

OSIP. Only he won't go to you . . . he's with his wife now.

ANNA. Go on, what do you know about it? . . . Good-bye, you murderer! (*She runs off.*)

OSIP (*flinging his cap down on the ground and weeping*). It's over! It's all over, may the earth swallow it all up! I saw it all, I heard it! My eyes were popping out of my head, it was like a great hammer beating at my ears! I heard it all. Well, how can I do anything else but kill him, seeing as I want to tear him up into little pieces, eat him . . . (*He sits down on the embankment with his back to the schoolhouse.*) I've got to kill him . . . kill him . . . (*He goes off.*)

PLATONOV (*thrusting* NIKOLAI TRILETSKI *out of the schoolhouse*). Out! Off with you to the shopkeeper's this very instant! Quick march!

NIKOLAI TRILETSKI (*stretching himself*). I'd rather you'd have given me a good caning tomorrow than wake me now!

PLATONOV. And what if the shopkeeper's dead already?

NIKOLAI TRILETSKI. If he's dead, then the kingdom of heaven be his, and if he's still continuing the struggle for existence, you're wrong to say such terrible things! I'm not going to the shopkeeper's! I want to go to sleep!

PLATONOV. You are going, you brute, you are! (*Pushing him.*) I shan't let you sleep! What do you think you're at? What are you playing at? Why aren't you doing anything? You do nothing but stuff yourself with food all the time! Why aren't you continuing your studies? Why aren't you reading your medical books, you animal?

NIKOLAI TRILETSKI. Listen, Mikhail Vasilyevich, who gave you the right to go thrusting your great cold paws into the hearts of others? . . .

PLATONOV. No, we'll produce nothing but a rash on the face of the earth! We're a lost people, we're not worth a farthing! (*Weeping.*) There isn't a single one . . . It's all vulgar . . . filthy . . . shop-soiled . . . Get away with you, Nikolai! Go!

NIKOLAI TRILETSKI (*shrugging his shoulders*). Are you crying? (*Pause.*) I'll go to the shopkeeper. Do you hear? I'll go!

PLATONOV. Do as you wish . . .

NIKOLAI TRILETSKI. I'll go! Look, I'm going now . . .

PLATONOV (*stamping his feet*). Get away!

NIKOLAI TRILETSKI. All right . . . You go to bed, Michel! It's not worth worrying about! Good-bye! (*He begins to move off, then stops.*) Just one word of farewell. I'd like you to advise all preachers, including yourself, to see that the sermons fit in with the preacher's deeds . . . One ought to give you a fearful beating, smash you up into little pieces and break with you for ever for what you did to that girl! . . . But I don't know how! I'm not much of a duellist! That's your good luck! . . . (*Pause.*) Good-bye! (*He goes out.*)

PLATONOV (*after a pause*). Shall I go? . . . To go or not to go? (*He sighs.*) I'll go . . . I'll go and strike up that long and essentially boring, ugly song . . . And I thought that I went about in armour that was secure! What happens? A woman just says the word and it's like a hurricane let loose inside me . . . For others it's questions of world importance, but for me it's – woman! The whole of my life boils down to one thing – woman! For Caesar it was the Rubicon, for me – woman . . . I'm just a skirt-chaser, nothing more! It wouldn't be so bad if I didn't struggle. But I do struggle! I'm weak, infinitely weak!

SASHA (*appearing at the window*). Misha, are you there?

PLATONOV. I'm here, my poor little treasure!

SASHA. Come inside!

PLATONOV. No, Sasha! I want to stay out in the fresh air! My head's splitting. Go and sleep, my angel!

SASHA. Good night! (*She shuts the window.*)

PLATONOV. It's hard to swindle someone whose faith is boundless! It makes me sweat and blush . . . I'm off! (*He moves off. He meets, coming in the opposite direction,* KATYA *and* YAKOV. *As he catches sight of* KATYA.) You? What do you want?

KATYA (*who is frightened*). Ah . . . It's you? I was looking for you.

PLATONOV. Is it you, Katya? All of them, from the lady right down to the chambermaid, they're all night birds! What do you want?

KATYA (*quietly*). I've a letter for you from the mistress.

PLATONOV. Which mistress?

KATYA (*quieter*). From Sofya Yegorovna . . .

PLATONOV. What? Have you gone mad? Go and douse yourself with cold water!

KATYA (*handing him the letter*). Here it is!

PLATONOV (*snatching it*). Letter . . . Letter . . . What letter? Couldn't you have brought it in the morning? (*He unseals it.*) Can't see to read it . . .

KATYA. Her ladyship would like a reply as quickly as possible . . .

PLATONOV (*lighting a match*). To hell with you all! (*He reads.*) 'Am taking the first step . . . Come, let's take it together . . . Am being resurrected . . . Come and take me . . . I'm yours . . .' What the devil! Just like a telegram! 'Shall wait till four in summer-house near the four posts . . . Husband drunk, gone off hunting with young Glagolyev. All yours. S.' My God! This is the last straw! (*To* KATYA.) What are you looking at?

KATYA. Why shouldn't I look if I've got eyes in my head?

PLATONOV. Put your eyes out then! You're sure it's for me, this letter?

KATYA. Quite sure, sir . . .

PLATONOV. You're lying! Clear out!

KATYA. Very good, sir. (*She goes off with* YAKOV.)

PLATONOV (*after a pause*). Well, that's the outcome for you . . . You're in it now, my boy! You've mutilated a woman, a living being, just for a lark, without any rhyme or reason, without any need for it at all . . . (*He thinks.*) I'll go away! Go away immediately! Quick march out of here to the four corners of the earth and submit to the iron rule of poverty and labour! (*A pause.*) I'll go away . . . But . . . is it really possible that Sofya loves me? (*He laughs; a pause.*) Strange . . . Is it really possible that this splendid marble statue of a woman with her wonderful hair is capable of falling in love with a poverty-stricken eccentric like me? Is she really in love? Incredible! (*He lights a *match and reads over the letter; he begins to laugh.*) This is a new life, with new characters, with new scenery! Yes, I'll go! Quick march to the summer-house near the four posts! Just you wait, my Sofya! You were mine and you will be mine! (*He begins to go, then he stops.*) I shan't go! (*He comes back.*) Break up my family? (*Shouting.*) Sasha, I'm coming in! Open up! (*Clutching his head.*) I shan't go, I shan't go . . . I shan't go! (*Pause.*) I will go! (*He moves off.*) Go, smash, trample, defile! (*He collides with* VOINITSEV *and* KIRIL GLAGOLYEV. *Both have rifles slung over their shoulders.*)

VOINITSEV. Here he is! Here he is! (*Embracing* PLATONOV.) Well? How about coming to the hunt with us?

PLATONOV. No . . . Wait!

VOINITSEV. Why do you tear yourself away, friend? (*He laughs.*) Drunk, I'm drunk! For the first time in my life, I'm drunk! Oh my God, how happy I am! My dear friend! (*He embraces* PLATONOV.) Shall we go? Sophie sent me off . . . Ordered me to shoot her some game . . .

KIRIL GLAGOLYEV. Let's go quickly! It's getting light already . . .

VOINITSEV. Have you heard what we've thought up? A stroke of genius, isn't it? We're thinking of putting on *Hamlet*! Word of honour!

PLATONOV. Let go . . . I'm drunk . . .

VOINITSEV. Wait . . . It's my idea! We'll start straight away tomorrow painting the scenery! I shall play Hamlet, Sophie will play Ophelia, you – Claudius, Triletski – Horatio . . . Oh, I'm so happy! So contented! Shakespeare, Sophie, you and maman! I don't need anything else! No wait, Glinka too! Nothing else! I shall be Hamlet . . . 'A murderer and a villain; A slave that is not twentieth part the tithe of your precedent lord . . .' What a Hamlet, eh?

PLATONOV (*tears himself away and runs*). Scoundrel! (*He runs off.*)

VOINITSEV. Ho, ho! He *is* drunk! (*He laughs.*) What do you think of our friend, eh?

KIRIL GLAGOLYEV. He's pickled . . . Let's go!

VOINITSEV. Let's go! . . . 'Give me that man – That is not passion's slave, and I will wear him – In my heart's core . . .' 'Fair Ophelia – Nymph, in thy orisons be all my sins remembered' . . . (*They go off. The sound of an approaching train is heard.*)

OSIP *runs in, looks around, takes the gun from his shoulder and fires into the air.* SASHA *appears at the window.*

SASHA. What's that?

OSIP. All is lost, Alexandra Ivanovna! Mikhail Vasilyevich, he's gone to her, to the general's lady! She was here calling him to go back with her! Now he's gone off to her, damn him.

SASHA. You're lying!

OSIP. May the Lord punish me, he's gone to her! I heard and saw everything! They were hugging and kissing here . . .

SASHA. You're lying!

OSIP. Let neither my father nor my mother see the kingdom of heaven if I'm lying! He's gone off to her! He's left his wife! Go and catch him up, Alexandra Ivanovna! No, no . . . It's all up! And now you are the unfortunate one! Let her meet him! (*He throws his gun down on to the ground.*) I'll cut his throat, Alexandra Ivanovna. (*He jumps over the embankment and sits on the stump.*) Don't worry, Alexandra Ivanovna . . . don't worry . . . I'll cut his throat . . .Make no mistake . . .

The lights of the oncoming train appear.

SASHA (*coming out in her nightdress, her hair down and in disorder*). He's gone . . . He's deceived me . . . (*She sobs.*) I'm lost . . . Kill me, Lord, after this . . . (*The train whistle is heard.*) I'll lie down in front of the engine . . . I don't want to live . . . (*She lies down on the rails.*) He deceived me. Kill, me, Mother of God! (*Pause.*) Lord, forgive me . . . Lord, forgive me . . . (*Crying out.*) Kolya! (*She gets up on her knees.*) My son! Save him! Save him! It's coming! It's here! Save him!

OSIP *jumps up and runs to her.*

SASHA (*falling on to the rails*). Ah . . .

OSIP (*picking her up and carrying her into the schoolhouse*). I'll cut his throat . . . Don't worry!

The train passes through.

Curtain

Act Three

A room in the schoolhouse. There are doors right and left. A cupboard with crockery, a chest of drawers, an old upright piano, chairs, a couch upholstered in oilcloth, a guitar etc., a state of utter untidiness.

PLATONOV *is asleep on the couch, by the window. His face is covered with a straw hat.*

SOFYA (*waking* PLATONOV). Platonov! Mikhail Vasilyevich! (*She pushes him.*) Wake up! Michel! (*Taking the hat from his face.*) How can you cover your face with such a dirty old hat? Ugh, the filth! What a sloven! He's lost his studs, he's sleeping there with his shirt wide open! He's unwashed and the shirt's a disgrace! . . . Michel! I'm speaking to you! Get up!

PLATONOV. Eh?

SOFYA. Wake up!

PLATONOV. Later . . . All right . . .

SOFYA. That'll do now! Get up, will you!

PLATONOV. Who is it? (*Rising.*) It's you, is it, Sofya?

SOFYA (*holding a watch right up to his face*). Just take a look!

PLATONOV. All right . . . (*He lies down again.*)

SOFYA. Platonov!

PLATONOV. Oh, what do you want? (*Rising.*) Eh? (SOFYA *thrusts the watch into his face again.*) Half past seven.

SOFYA. Half past seven . . . And have you forgotten our arrangement?

PLATONOV. What arrangement?

SOFYA. What arrangement? You've forgotten, have you?

What's the matter with you? Your eyes are red, you're all crumpled . . . Are you sick? (*Pause.*) The arrangement was this: both of us were to be at the hut at six o'clock this morning . . . Have you forgotten? It's long past six . . .

PLATONOV. Go on . . .

SOFYA (*sitting down beside him*). Aren't you even ashamed? Why didn't you come? You gave your word of honour . . .

PLATONOV. And I would have kept my word if I hadn't fallen asleep . . . You can see I've been sleeping, can't you? So why do you keep on pestering me? . . .

SOFYA. It's three weeks since that night and never, never once have you arrived on time for a single one of our meetings.

PLATONOV. I'm very happy to hear it!

SOFYA. That's not clever, Platonov! You ought to be ashamed! Why is it that when I am with you, you lose all your sense of nobility, you cease to be intelligent, you no longer seem to be yourself? Why this plebeian horseplay, so unworthy of the man to whom I owe the salvation of my spiritual life? You conduct yourself in my presence like some kind of freak . . . Not a kind look, not a gentle word, not even a single word of love! . . . Here I come to see you – and you smell of liquor, your clothes are a disgrace, your hair isn't brushed, you're rude, your answers are disjointed . . .

PLATONOV (*jumping up and striding about*). She's off! . . .

SOFYA. Are you drunk?

PLATONOV. What business is that of yours?

SOFYA. How nice! (*She weeps.*)

PLATONOV. Women!

SOFYA. What are you doing to me? (*She rises.*) Thanks to you, I'm a sick woman! Day and night I have a pain in my chest, thanks to you! Don't you see all this? You don't even want to? You hate me! If you loved me, you wouldn't dare treat me like this! I'm not some simple peasant wench or other, I'm no coarse, uncouth creature . . . I'm not going to allow any kind of a fellow like you . . . (*She sits.*) For God's sake! (*She weeps.*)

PLATONOV. That's enough!

SOFYA. Why are you killing me? Where is the happiness you promised me? How is this all going to end? Think, Platonov, before it's too late! Think, think now . . . Sit down here on this chair, put everything out of your head and just think of one thing: what are you doing to me?

PLATONOV. I don't know how to think. (*Pause.*) But now *you* think! (*He comes up to her.*) You think! I've deprived you of your family, your happiness, your future . . . Why? I've robbed you as if I were your most bitter enemy! What can I give you in return? It's your misfortune, this sordid liaison of ours, your downfall! (*He sits down.*)

SOFYA. I have united myself with him and he dares call this a sordid liaison!

PLATONOV. I've destroyed you, that's all there is to it! And not only you . . . Wait and see what tune your husband will strike up when he finds out!

SOFYA. You're afraid he might make things unpleasant for you?

PLATONOV. I'm afraid that we might kill him . . .

SOFYA. Then why did you come to me, you lily-livered coward, if you knew that we were going to kill him?

PLATONOV. If you don't mind . . . a little less . . . pathos! You won't get at my heart strings with your chest notes . . . And why did you . . . However . . . (*he gestures with his hand*) talking with you only means shedding your tears . . .

SOFYA. Yes, yes . . . I never wept before I began to live with you! Go on then, be afraid, tremble! He already knows!

PLATONOV. What?

SOFYA. He already knows. (PLATONOV *rises.*) Yes . . . I told him about it all this morning . . .

PLATONOV. You're joking . . .

SOFYA. You've turned pale, have you? One ought to hate

you, not love you! I must be mad . . . I just don't know why . . . why I love you. He already knows! (*She shakes him by the sleeve.*) He knows all! . . . (*Pause.*)

PLATONOV. What did he say?

SOFYA. At first he thought I was joking, but when he became convinced that I wasn't, he turned pale, began to sway, burst into tears, started to crawl about on his knees . . . He had the very same repulsive face that you have now!

PLATONOV. What have you done, you loathsome woman? (*Seizing his head in his hands.*) You've killed him! And you dare to speak of it so cold-bloodedly! You've killed him! Did you . . . name me?

SOFYA. Yes . . . How else? . . .

PLATONOV. And he? . . .

SOFYA (*jumping up*). Really, have you no shame, Platonov? You don't know what you're saying! So, according to you, I shouldn't have spoken?

PLATONOV. No! (*He lies face down on the couch.*)

SOFYA. What are you saying? I was bound to tell him! I am an honest woman!

PLATONOV. Do you know what you've done by telling him? You've parted with your husband for ever!

SOFYA. Yes . . . for ever! How else could it be? Platonov, you're beginning to talk like a . . . scoundrel!

PLATONOV. For ever . . . And what will happen to you when we part? And part we shall soon! You'll be the first to see the error of your ways; then you'll leave me! (*He gestures with his hand.*) However . . . do as you like, Sofya! You're honest and clever . . . more than I am . . . So you can take charge of the whole of this pointless mess. Say and do as you like, I leave it all to you! Resurrect me if you can, raise me up on my feet again! Only quickly, for God's sake, or I'll go mad!

SOFYA. We leave here tomorrow!

PLATONOV. Yes, yes, let's leave . . . only quickly!

SOFYA. I must take you away from here . . . I've written to my mother about you. We'll go to her . . .

PLATONOV. Wherever you like! . . . Do as you think best!

SOFYA. Michel! Why, this is our new life! . . . My head is clearer than yours! Believe me, my dearest! I'll raise you up on your feet again! I'll take you to where there's more light, where there isn't any of this squalor, this dust, this sloth, this filthy shirt . . . I'll make a man of you . . . I'll give you happiness! We'll be real people, Michel! We'll eat our own bread, we'll pour out our sweat, have callouses on our hands . . . (*She rests her head on his breast.*) I shall work . . .

PLATONOV. Where will you work? You don't know how to work. What kind of work will you do?

SOFYA. You'll see! Believe me, Michel! I shall light the way for you! You have resurrected me and I will give the whole of my life up to you in gratitude . . . Do we leave tomorrow? Yes? I'll go now and start packing . . . And you get ready too . . . Come to the hut at ten o'clock and bring your things with you . . . You'll come?

PLATONOV. I'll come . . .

SOFYA. Give me your word of honour that you'll come!

PLATONOV. A-a-a . . . I said I'd come!

SOFYA. Give me your word of honour!

PLATONOV. My word of honour . . . as God's my witness . . .

SOFYA (*laughing*). I believe, I believe! Come even earlier . . . I'll be ready before ten, And we'll drive off by night! We'll start to live, Michel! You don't understand your own good fortune, you silly man! You'll be another man tomorrow, fresh, new! We'll begin to breathe a new air; a new blood will start coursing through our veins . . . (*She laughs.*) Away with the old man! Here, take my hand! Shake it! (*She extends her hand;* PLATONOV *kisses it.*) Good-bye for the present! I'll get ready quickly! . . . (*She kisses him.*)

PLATONOV. Good-bye . . . Did you say ten or eleven?

SOFYA. Ten . . . Even earlier. And put some decent clothes on for the journey . . . (*She laughs.*) I have some cash . . . We'll have supper somewhere on the way! I'll go and get ready. Cheer up then! I expect you at ten! (*She runs off.*)

PLATONOV (*after a pause*). It's not a new tune . . . I've heard it a hundred times . . . (*Pause.*) Farewell Voinitsevka! Farewell all! Both Sasha and the general's widow . . . (*He opens the cupboard.*) I'm a new man tomorrow! Terribly new! (He *pours out some wine and drinks it.*) What am I going to take my clothes in? I haven't a suitcase . . . Did I drink just then? Why? I shan't drink any more . . . It's the last time . . . I'll write to Sasha . . . (*He lies down on the couch.*) Sofya believes so sincerely . . . Blessed are they that believe! . . . Laugh, madame la générale! She will laugh, too! She'll laugh loudly! Yes! I think there was a letter from her . . . where is it? (*He takes a letter from the window.*) The hundredth, if not the two hundredth letter since that savage night . . . (*Reading.*) 'You, Platonov, who have not answered my letters, are an indelicate, cruel, stupid ignoramus! One would think that you were ashamed of that night! If you're not going to pay any attention to this letter too, then so be it, I'll have to come to you myself, damn you! All day long I wait! It's stupid, Platonov! Au revoir!' (*Pause.*) What handwriting! Neat, bold . . . Commas, full stops . . . A woman who can spell and punctuate is a pretty rare phenomenon! . . . (MARKO *enters.*) I'd better write her a letter or I suppose she will come here . . . (*Catching sight of* MARKO.) Well, and here's another phenomenon . . . Come in, please! Who are you looking for?

MARKO. I've come to see your lordship. (*He takes a summons out of his satchel.*) I've got a summons here for your grace . . .

PLATONOV. Ah, that's very nice. What summons? Who are you from?

MARKO. From Ivan Andreyevich, the Justice of the Peace . . .

PLATONOV. Hm . . . From the J.P.? What does he want with me? Give it here! (*Taking the summons.*) Invitation to another christening, is it? (*He reads.*) '. . . as defendant in the case of assault and battery committed on the person of Marya Yefimovna Grekova, Councillor of State's daughter . . .' (*He laughs.*) I'll be damned! Bravo! When is the case to be heard? The day after tomorrow? I'll come, I'll come . . . Tell him I'll come . . . Good for her, by God, good for her!

MARKO. Would you sign for it, sir.

PLATONOV. Sign for it? Certainly . . . Brother, you look terribly like a wounded duck!

MARKO. Begging your pardon, I don't look like anything of the sort, sir . . .

PLATONOV (*sitting down at the table*). What do you look like then?

MARKO. The image and likeness of God, sir . . .

PLATONOV. U-huh . . . Artillery man, are you?

MARKO. That's correct, sir . . . I was discharged after the Sebastopol campaign, sir . . . Spent four years in hospital over and above the ordinary run of service . . . I was a sergeant, sir.

PLATONOV. U-huh . . . Cannon were all right, were they?

MARKO. The usual ones . . . Round bore . . .

PLATONOV (*rising*). Take it. I've signed five times. What a clever girl she is, by God! I didn't expect it of her, I really didn't! And who are the witnesses? Who else have you got summonses for?

MARKO (*reads*). 'Doctor Nikolai Ivanovich Triletski,' sir. (PLATONOV *laughs.*) 'Mr. Kiril Porfirich Glagolyev, Mr. Sergei Pavlovich Voinitsev, graduate of the St. Petersburg neversity . . .'

PLATONOV. Is that how it's written there, 'neversity'?

MARKO. No, not at all . . .

PLATONOV. Then why do you read it that way?

MARKO. It's because I'm ignorant, sir . . .

PLATONOV. Hm . . . All this is the day after tomorrow, and tomorrow we have to leave . . . Pity, I can imagine what kind of a case it would make! (*He starts to walk about.*) Pity . . .

MARKO. Wouldn't your lordship be wanting to give me something for a cup of tea?

PLATONOV. Eh?

MARKO. Something for a cup of tea . . . I've had to walk a long way.

PLATONOV. You don't want a cup of tea . . . But what am I saying? All right, my dear fellow! I can't give you anything for a cup of tea, but I'll give you some tea instead . . . I can afford that, and what's more, it'll keep you sober . . . (*He takes a tea caddy out of the cupboard.*) Here . . . It's good tea, nice and strong . . . What am I going to put it in for you?

MARKO (*presenting his pocket*). Just put it in there . . .

PLATONOV. Straight into your pocket? Won't it smell?

MARKO. Put it in, put it in . . . Don't you worry about that . . .

PLATONOV (*pouring the tea leaves into his pocket*). Enough?

MARKO. Thank you kindly . . .

PLATONOV. Wait . . . One moment . . . (*He sits down and writes on the summons.*) 'Then I kissed you because . . . because I was irritated and didn't know what I wanted, but now I'd kiss you as though you were some sacred shrine. It was foul, the way I treated you, I admit it. I'm foul to everyone. I'm afraid we won't be meeting at the court. Tomorrow I'm leaving for good. I wish you every happiness and that you at least will be just and fair towards me. Don't forgive me!' (*To* MARKO.) Do you know where Grekova lives?

MARKO. I do, sir. It's quite a way. You have to cross the river at the ford.

PLATONOV. That's right. Take this letter to her and you'll get three roubles. Give it to the young lady personally . . . I don't want any reply . . . If she tries to give you one, don't take it . . . Take it to her today . . . Right now . . . (*He walks up and down.*)

MARKO. I understand.

PLATONOV. What else? Yes! Tell everyone that I've begged Grekova's forgiveness and that she's refused to forgive me.

MARKO. I understand. A good day to you!

PLATONOV. Good-bye, friend! Keep well!

MARKO *goes out.*

PLATONOV (*alone*). So we're quits with Grekova! She'll see that my name is mud throughout the whole length and breadth of the province. And that's how it should be! For the first time in my life I'm punished by a woman. (*He lies down.*) You play dirty tricks on them and they cling to your neck! Sofya, for example . . . (*He covers his face with a handkerchief.*) You used to be as free as the wind and now . . . lie here . . . wait . . . daydream . . . Love! . . . Amo, amas, amat! (*Sighing.*) Poor Voinitsevs! And Sasha? Poor girl! What's she going to do without me? She'll pine, she'll die . . . She's gone, she sensed the truth . . . Gone with the child without saying a single word . . . She left that very same night . . . I ought to go and say good-bye to her . . .

ANNA (*at the window*). Can I come in? Hey! Is anyone there?

PLATONOV. Anna Petronva! (*He jumps up and begins to straighten himself.*)

ANNA (*at the window*). Can I come in? I'm coming in! Do you hear?

PLATONOV (*combing his hair*). I'll have a drink before she comes in! (*He quickly opens the cupboard and drinks quickly.*) God, what if she knows? . . .

ANNA *enters.* PLATONOV *slowly closes the cupboard.*

ANNA. *My humble respects to you!*

PLATONOV. It won't shut . . . (*Pause.*) Ah . . . is that you, Anna Petrovna? I didn't notice . . . It just will not shut . . . Strange . . . (*He drops the key and picks it up again.*)

ANNA. Well, come over here to me then! Leave the cupboard alone. Leave it!

PLATONOV (*coming up to her*). Hello . . .

ANNA. Why won't you look at me?

PLATONOV. I'm ashamed to . . . (*He kisses her hand.*)

ANNA. Hm . . . Have you seduced anybody?

PLATONOV. Yes, something like that . . .

ANNA. Bravo, Platonov! But who then?

PLATONOV. I shan't tell you . . .

ANNA. Let's sit down . . . (*She sits down on the couch.*) We'll find out, young man, we'll find out . . . But why be ashamed in front of me! After all, I've known your sinful soul for a long time now . . .

PLATONOV. Don't ask me, Anna Petrovna! I'm not in the mood today for being present at my own cross-examination. Speak, if you wish, but don't ask me any questions!

ANNA. Very well. Did you get my letters?

PLATONOV. Yes.

ANNA. Then why haven't you come?

PLATONOV. I can't.

ANNA. Sulking?

PLATONOV. No. Why should I sulk? Don't ask me, for God's sake!

ANNA. Sit up properly, now! Why haven't you come to see me these past three weeks?

PLATONOV. I've been sick.

ANNA. You're lying!

PLATONOV. Yes, I'm lying. Don't ask me why, Anna Petrovna!

ANNA. Hm . . . Drinking! Last year's business all over again! Last year you seduced someone and the whole summer you went round looking like a wet hen! Don Juan and a pitiful coward all rolled into one! Don't you dare drink! (*She gets up.*) Where is it? (PLATONOV *points to the cupboard.*) Shame on you, Misha! Where's your strength of character? (*She opens the cupboard.*) The mess! Alexandra Ivanovna will be giving you a piece of her mind when she returns! Do you want your wife to return? Why, it's a regular tavern you've got here in your cupboard! (*She takes a sip out of a bottle.*) It's good . . . Come on then, let's have a little drink, shall we? Just one and then we won't drink any more! (PLATONOV *goes to the cupboard.*) Hold the glass! (*She pours.*) Put that one down the hatch! I shan't give you any more! (PLATONOV *drinks.*) Now I'll have one too . . . (*She pours.*) Here's to all sinners! (*She drinks.*) That's you! Excellent stuff! You're quite a connoisseur! (*She hands him the bottle.*) Here! Bring it over here! (*They go to the window.*) Now say good-bye to your delicious drink! (*She looks through the window.*) It's a pity to throw it out! Shall we have another drink, eh? Shall we?

PLATONOV. As you like . . .

ANNA (*pouring*). Drink up . . . Quickly now!

PLATONOV (*drinking*). Your health! God grant you happiness!

ANNA (*pouring and drinking herself*). Did you miss me? Let's sit down, shall we? (*They sit down.*) Did you miss me?

PLATONOV. Every moment.

ANNA. Why didn't you come then?

PLATONOV. Don't ask me! I shan't tell you anything, not because I'm not frank with you, but because I refuse to offend your ears! I'm lost, altogether lost, my dearest! Pangs of conscience, depression, despondency . . . in short, torment! Now that you've come, I begin to feel better.

ANNA. You're all thin, you look sick . . . I cannot abide these romantic heroes! What are you playing at, Platonov? Which novel is he from, this hero that you're acting?

Despondency, melancholy, the struggle of the passions, love with prefaces . . .

PLATONOV. It's easy enough to say that . . . But what can one do?

ANNA. In the first place, live like a human being, that is, don't drink, don't loll about all day long, wash yourself more often, come to see me . . . (*She stands up.*) Come over to my house now!

PLATONOV. What? (*He stands up.*) Go to your house? No, no . . .

ANNA. Come on! You'll see people, you'll be able to talk, you'll listen, quarrel . . . Why not?

PLATONOV. Don't ask me! I can't, that's all!

ANNA. Of course you can! Put your hat on! Come on!

PLATONOV. I can't, Anna Petrovna! Not for anything in the world! I'm not going a step out of this house!

ANNA (*putting his hat on to his head*). Stop playing the fool, Platonov. Come on, quick march! Michel, what's the matter?

PLATONOV (*tearing himself away*). Why do you pester me? I've said, haven't I, that I will not go! Kindly permit me to do as I like! (*Pause.*) I will not go!

ANNA. Look here, Platonov . . . I'll lend you a little money and you go away somewhere for a month, or even two . . .

PLATONOV. Where?

ANNA. Moscow, Petersburg . . . All right? Do that, Michel! It's absolutely essential for you to have an airing! You'll have a nice trip, see people, go to the theatre . . . It'll be such a refreshing change for you! I'll give you money, letters . . . Would you like me to come with you? Would you like that? We'd have a really fine time! And then we'll come back here restored, radiant . . .

PLATONOV. A delightful idea, but unfortunately it's not feasible . . . I leave here tomorrow, Anna Petrovna, but not with you!

ANNA. As you wish . . . Where are you going?

PLATONOV. I'm leaving . . . (*Pause.*) I'm leaving this place for good.

ANNA. Nonsense . . . (*She drinks from the bottle.*) Poppycock!

PLATONOV. I'll disappear for good . . . (*He takes her by the sleeve, then by the shoulder.*) Forget the fool, the ass, the scoundrel, the villain Platonov. The earth will swallow him up, he'll vanish completely. Perhaps, many, many years later, we'll meet again, when both of us will be able to laugh and shed our elderly tears over these days, but now . . . to hell with them! (*He kisses her hand.*)

ANNA. Here, have a drink! (*She pours the wine for him.*) It's no crime to talk balderdash when you're drunk . . .

PLATONOV (*drinking*). Go on, laugh, you wonderful, radiant, intelligent woman! Tomorrow I run away from here, I run away from myself, I run away to a new life! So it's good-bye for good . . .

ANNA. Hm . . . You'll be lost without me, Platonov! (*Rubbing her forehead.*) I'm a little tipsy . . . Let's leave together!

PLATONOV. No . . . Tomorrow you'll find out about everything . . . (*He turns away to the window.*)

ANNA. Do you need money?

PLATONOV. No . . . (*He turns to her.*) Go away, Anna Petrovna, or God knows what I'll do! I'll burst into sobs, I'll beat myself and . . . Go away! It's impossible for me to stay! I'm telling you in plain Russian . . . Do try and understand! Why do you look at me like that? (ANNA *gives him her hand; he kisses it.*) Go, my dearest . . . (*He kisses her hand.*) Good-bye . . . Leave me . . . (*He covers his face with her hand.*)

ANNA. You've gone all soft and sentimental, my sweetheart . . . Well? Let go my hand . . . Good-bye! Let's have a farewell drink, what? (*She pours.*) There! . . . Bon voyage and may happiness be waiting for you at the other end! (*They drink.*) Another one to drown your sorrows? (*She pours.*) Oh, damn it all!

PLATONOV (*drinking*). May you have every happiness! Go on living here . . . You can do without me.

ANNA. If we're going to drink, we might as well do it properly. (*She pours.*) If you drink you die and if you don't drink you die, so you might as well die drinking . . . (*She drinks.*) I'm a drunkard, Platonov . . . (*She sits down.*) There's nothing worse than being an educated woman . . . She may be educated, but she's idle . . . (*Pause.*) I'm involuntarily immoral . . . I'm an immoral woman, Platonov . . . (*She laughs.*) Eh? And perhaps that's why I love you, because I'm immoral . . . (*She rubs her brow.*) And I'll perish . . . Such women always perish . . . I ought to be made a professor somewhere, or a director . . . If I were a diplomat I'd turn the whole world upside down . . . She may be educated, but she's . . . idle . . . I'm just not needed, I suppose . . . Why don't you say something, eh?

PLATONOV. We're both of us in a bad way . . .

ANNA. If only one had children . . . Do you like children? (*She rises.*) Stay, darling! Won't you stay? We'd have such good times! Michel, I want to be . . . a wife, a mother . . . (*Pause.*) Don't be silent! Say something! Won't you stay?

PLATONOV (*looking out of the window*). I'll kill myself if I stay.

ANNA. But you do love me?

PLATONOV. Go away, can't you, or I'll tell you everything, and if I do that, I'll kill myself! (*Pause;* ANNA *offers him her hand.*)

ANNA. I'm offering you my hand . . . Don't you see?

PLATONOV. You'll never see me again . . . (*He embraces and kisses her.*) For the last time . . . (*He pushes her through the door.*) Good-bye! Good luck! (*He bolts the door.*)

ANNA (*through the door*). I swear to God that we'll see each other again!

PLATONOV. No! Good-bye! (*He stuffs his fingers into his ears.*) I can't hear anything! Be quiet and go away! I've stopped up my ears!

ANNA. I'm going! I'll send Sergei to you and I give you my word that you won't leave and if you leave, it'll be with me! Good-bye!

A pause.

PLATONOV (*alone*). Has she gone? (*He goes to the door and listens.*) She's gone. Or perhaps not? (*He opens the door.*) She's a devil . . . (*He looks out through the door.*) She's gone . . . (*He lies down on the couch.*) Good-bye my dearest! (*Sighing.*) And I'll never see her again . . . (*Pause.*) What if I ask Sofya to put off our departure for two weeks or so? Then I could go off with Anna! That's right! Only two weeks . . . Sofya will agree . . . She can stay with her mother for the time being . . . I'll ask her, eh? While I'm away with Anna, Sofya can have a rest, regain her strength . . . After all, I wouldn't be going away for ever! (*There is a knock at the door.*) I'll go! It's decided! Capital! . . . (*There is another knock.*) Who's that? Is she back? Who's there? (*Another knock.*) Is that you? (*He rises.*) I won't let her in! (*He goes to the door.*) Is it she? (*Another knock.*) She's giggling, I think . . . (*He laughs.*) It is she . . . I must let her in . . . (*He opens the door.*) Ah! (OSIP *enters.*) What's all this? You, you devil? Why have you come?

OSIP. Good day, Mikhail Vasilyevich!

PLATONOV. Well I never! To what and to whom do I owe the honour of being visited by such an important personage? Say what you have to say quickly and get to hell out of here!

OSIP. I'll sit down . . . (*He sits down.*)

PLATONOV. Please do, I shall count it as a favour! (*A pause;* PLATONOV *sits down beside him.*) Why have you come?

OSIP. To say good-bye.

PLATONOV. Are you going away?

OSIP. I'm not going away, but you are.

PLATONOV. Is that so! And how do you know?

OSIP. How do you think?

PLATONOV. You're a magician, Osip. I am going away, dear fellow. You're right.

OSIP. There you are! So, you see, I know. I even know where you're going!

PLATONOV. Yes? Think of that now! I don't know. You're a man of great wisdom, there's no denying it! Well then, tell me, where am I going?

OSIP. To the next world.

PLATONOV. Long way! (*Pause.*) Hm . . . So you've come to kill me, have you?

OSIP. That's right . . .

PLATONOV (*mocking*). That's right . . . Damn your impertinence! Hm . . . Is this your own decision or are you doing it on someone's behalf?

OSIP (*showing him a twenty-five rouble note*). Here . . . Old Vengerovich gave me this to cripple your grace! (*He tears the note up.*) That's so that you shouldn't think when you're in the next world that I killed you for money. (PLATONOV *gets up and walks about.*) Are you afraid, Mikhail Vasilyevich? Scared, are you? (*He laughs.*) Run! Shout! I'm not standing by the door, I'm not holding it: there's a way out. Go and call the people together, say that Osip has come to kill you! Because he has come to kill you . . . You don't believe me? (*Pause.*)

PLATONOV (*going up to* OSIP *and looking at him*). Amazing! (*Pause.*) Why are you smiling? Fool! (*Strikes him on the arm.*) Don't you dare smile! You're being spoken to! Silence! I'll see that you hang! I'll tear you into little pieces, brigand! (*Quickly moving away from him.*) However . . . Don't annoy me! I mustn't be annoyed . . . I get this pain . . .

OSIP. Go on, slap me on the face for being a bad man!

PLATONOV. As much as you like! (*He comes up to* OSIP *and slaps his face.*) Scoundrel! (*Again he slaps his face.*) Filth! I'll . . . you . . . (*Quickly moving away from* OSIP.) Get out!

OSIP. Go on, spit in my eyes for being a bad man!

PLATONOV. I wouldn't waste my spittle on you!

OSIP (*rising*). You dare to talk like that?

PLATONOV (*coming up to him*). You came to kill me, I think? Well, here I am! Go on, kill! Here I am! Kill me then!

OSIP. I respected you, Mr. Platonov, I held you as a fine man! But now . . . You're so very harmful . . . Why did the young lady come to see you today?

PLATONOV (*clutching him by the chest and shaking him*). Kill! Go on, Kill me!

OSIP. And why did the general's lady come after her? And where is your wife? Which of the three is your real wife? And will you tell me after all that that you're not a harmful man? (*He quickly trips him; they fall together to the floor and struggle.*) When you're in the next world, give my very humble respects to General Voinitsev!

PLATONOV. Let go!

OSIP (*taking a knife from his belt*). Keep still! I'm going to kill you whether you like it or not! Strong man, aren't you? Fine man! Don't feel like dying, do you? You shouldn't have touched what didn't belong to you!

PLATONOV (*shouting*). My arm! Stop, stop! My arm!

OSIP. Don't you feel like dying? In a moment you'll be in the kingdom of heaven . . .

PLATONOV. Not in the back, not in the back! Stab me in the chest! My arm, let go! My wife, my son . . . (SASHA *runs in.*)

SASHA. What's the matter? (*She shrieks.*) Misha! (*She runs over to the combatants and falls on top of them.*) What are you doing?

OSIP. Who's that? Alexandra Ivanovna? (*Jumping up.*) I'll let him go! (*To* SASHA.) Here's my knife! (*He gives her his knife.*) I shan't cut his throat in front of you . . . Let him live for the time being. I'll cut his throat later! He won't escape! (*He jumps out through the window.*)

PLATONOV (*after a pause*). The devil . . . Hello, Sasha! It's you, isn't it? (*He groans; she helps him up and over to the couch; he lies down.*)

SASHA. Here! (*Putting a cushion under his head.*) Like that! (*She sits at his feet.*) Does it hurt anywhere? (*Pause.*) Why have you shut your eyes?

PLATONOV. No, no . . . I was just . . . You've come, Sasha? You've come, my treasure? (*He kisses her hand.*)

SASHA. Little Kolya is ill.

PLATONOV. What's the matter with him?

SASHA. He coughs all the time, he's got a temperature and a rash . . . He hasn't slept for two nights now and he's been crying terribly all the time . . . He won't drink, he won't eat . . . (*Weeping.*) He's seriously ill, Misha! I'm so afraid for him . . .

PLATONOV. Don't worry, Sasha!

SASHA. How can I do anything else but worry? What if he dies, God forbid it! What will happen to us then?

PLATONOV (*sighing*). God won't take our little boy away from you! Why should he punish you? Unless it's for having married a good-for-nothing! (*Pause.*) Look after my little man for me, Sasha! Keep him safe and sound for me and I swear to you by all that's holy that I'll make a man of him! After all, the poor little mite, he's a Platonov too! I'm a paltry, insignificant man, I know, but I will be a splendid father! Oh, my arm! (*He groans.*) It's aching! It's badly bruised . . . (*Examining it.*) It's all red . . . Anyway, to hell with it! And so, Sasha . . . (*he embraces her head*) . . . why did you go away? Don't cry, my squirrel! Why all these tears? I do love you, you know, my little girl! I love you very much! I'm very much to blame, but you must forgive me . . . There, there . . .

SASHA. Is the affair over?

PLATONOV. Affair? What kind of a word is that, my little bourgeoise?

SASHA. So it isn't over?

PLATONOV. How shall I say? There isn't any affair, it's just a monstrous jumble of nonsense . . . If it's not over yet, it'll soon . . . be over!

SASHA. But when?

PLATONOV. Very soon. Soon we'll begin to live again, Sasha, as before! Damn all this nonsense about a new life! . . . She'll be the first to cool off . . . Sofya isn't a mate for me . . . She's no mate for me . . . (*Pause.*) Believe me! Sofya won't be your rival for long . . . Sasha, what's the matter with you? (SASHA *rises and sways;* PLATONOV *rises.*) Sasha!

SASHA. You're . . . you're . . . with Sofya and not Anna Petrovna?

PLATONOV. Is this the first you've heard of it?

SASHA. With Sofya? . . . It's vile . . . disgusting . . .

PLATONOV. What's the matter with you? (*He groans.*) Is this really news for you? Is this the first you've heard of it? . . .

SASHA. With the general's widow, it might just get by, but with someone else's wife! It's low, sinful . . . (*She goes to the door.*)

PLATONOV (*after a pause*). Shocked? But where are you going? Sasha! You've been reading too many silly novels . . .

SASHA. My God . . . Can this really be true? (*She puts her hands to her temples and sits down on the floor.*) I . . . I don't know what to do . . .

PLATONOV. Why start howling, my darling little silly? (*Pause.*) Oh, Sasha, Sasha . . . I've sinned terribly, I know, but is it really so impossible for you to forgive me?

SASHA. And have you forgiven yourself?

PLATONOV. A philosophical question! (*He kisses her on the head.*) What strange people you women are! Look, Sasha: you feed that scoundrel Osip, you won't let the cats and dogs have any peace with your ministrations, you sit up till midnight reciting interminable litanies for some supposed enemies of yours, so what does it cost you to throw a crust to your guilty, repentant husband? Why must you too be my executioner? Stay, Sasha! (*Embracing her.*) Who will love you as I do? (*He lifts her up.*) Who will lift you up like this? How can you exist without me, my treasure?

SASHA. I can't! Let me go! I'm lost! I'm lost and all you do is joke! (*She tears herself away.*) Think of what people will say! I won't be able to face them! (*Sobbing.*) You've broken up our home . . . (*She sits down.*) What have you done, Misha? (*She gets up.*) What have you done?

PLATONOV. Go then and God bless you!

SASHA. Good-bye! You won't see me again! Don't come to see us . . . Father will bring Kolya to visit you . . .

PLATONOV. Haven't you gone yet?

SASHA. I'm going . . . All right . . . (*She looks at* PLATONOV *for a while, then goes.*)

PLATONOV. And this is the man with a new life in front of him! It's aching! My God, an insect, a little louse like Sasha and even she . . . on the strength of some holiness or other she has the right to throw stones at me! Damn this kind of situation! (*He lies down;* VOINITSEV *enters and stops at the door. There is a pause.*) Is this the epilogue or is the comedy still in full swing? (*Having caught sight of* VOINITSEV, *he closes his eyes and begins to snore slightly.*)

VOINITSEV (*approaching* PLATONOV). Platonov! (*Pause.*) You're not asleep! I can see it by your face . . . (*He sits down beside him.*) I don't think that . . . you can sleep . . . (PLATONOV *gets up;* VOINITSEV *gets up and looks out of the window.*) You've killed me . . . Do you know that? (*There is a pause; he weeps.* PLATONOV *gets up and slowly goes to another corner of the room.*) For once in my life Fate presented me with a gift and . . . even that has been taken away! It didn't suffice him that he was intelligent, attractive, magnanimous . . . He needs must have my happiness as well! You've taken it away from me . . . And I? What am I? Nothing in particular . . . Huh . . . Not very strong, limited intelligence, effeminate, sentimental, god-forsaken . . . with an inclination to idleness, mysticism, superstition. . . Success is yours, friend!

PLATONOV. Go away from here!

VOINITSEV. In a minute . . . I was coming to challenge you to a duel . . . instead I come here and start to howl. I'm going . . . (*Pause.*) Have I lost her for good?

PLATONOV. Yes.

VOINITSEV (*whistling*). So . . . Naturally . . .

PLATONOV. Go away from here! I beg you! Go!

VOINITSEV. In a minute . . . (*He goes to the door; there is a pause.*) Give her back to me, Platonov! Save me, dear boy! Eh? Give her back to me! (*He sobs.*) After all, she's mine! Mine! Do you understand?

PLATONOV (*going to the couch*). Go away . . . I'll shoot myself . . . I swear on my honour . . .

VOINITSEV. No don't, don't do that, for God's sake! (*He gestures with his hand and goes.*)

PLATONOV (*seizing his head in his hands*). Oh, miserable wretch! Oh, my God! A curse on my god-forsaken head! (*He sobs.*) Keep away from people, you loathsome creature. I have brought misfortune to others and others have brought misfortune to me! They keep on slashing, slashing at me and still they can't manage to slay me! Under every chair, under each chip of wood there's a murderer sitting, looking into my eyes, seeking to slay me! Kill me then! (*Beating his breast.*) Kill me, before I do it myself! (*He runs to the door and shouts.*) Sasha! Sasha, for God's sake!

He opens the door; PORFIRI GLAGOLYEV *enters, muffled up and leaning on a crutch.*

PORFIRI GLAGOLYEV. You're in, Mikhail Vasilyevich? I'm so glad . . . I've disturbed you . . . Buy I shan't detain you,

I'll leave almost immediately . . . I just want to ask you one question. Give me your answer and I'll go. This question is of vital importance to me! I shall believe your answer because I know you to be a very honest man . . . I find myself in a terrible position! Our mutual friend . . . You know her well . . . So far I've considered her to be perfection in the human sense . . . Anna Petrovna Voinitseva . . . (*He supports* PLATONOV.) Don't fall, for God's sake! . . . Is she an honourable woman, Mikhail Vasilyevich? She . . . she . . . Has she the right to become the wife of an honourable man? (*Pause.*) I don't know how to formulate my question . . . Try to understand me, for God's sake! I've been told that she . . .

PLATONOV. All is vile, base, filthy in this world! . . . vile . . . (*He falls senseless against* PORFIRI GLAGOLYEV *and collapses in a heap on the floor.*)

KIRIL GLAGOLYEV (*entering*). Why are you dawdling about here? I'm not prepared to wait . . .

PORFIRI GLAGOLYEV. All is vile, base, filthy . . . including her too . . .

KIRIL GLAGOLYEV (*looking at* PLATONOV). Father, what's the matter with Platonov?

PORFIRI GLAGOLYEV. He's disgustingly drunk. Yes, vile, filthy . . . Profound, pitiless, stinging truth. (*Pause.*) We're going to Paris!

KIRIL GLAGOLYEV. What! to Pa . . . to Paris? What do you want to go to Paris for?

PORFIRI GLAGOLYEV. To wallow as this one is wallowing. (*Pointing to* PLATONOV.)

KIRIL GLAGOLYEV. Wallow . . . in Paris?

PORFIRI GLAGOLYEV. Enough! I'm not going to go on playing a part that interests no one but myself, bothering my head with ideals! There is no more faith, no more love! There are no more others, only myself! Let's go!

KIRIL GLAGOLYEV. To Paris?

PORFIRI GLAGOLYEV. Yes . . . If we're going to sin, let's do it in a foreign land, rather than our own. You be my teacher, son! To Paris!

KIRIL GLAGOLYEV. Now that is nice, father! You taught me to read, now I'm going to teach you to live! Come on!

They go.

Curtain

Act Four

The study of the late General Voinitsev. There are two doors. Old-fashioned furniture, Persian rugs, flowers. The walls are hung with rifles, pistols, daggers (of Caucasian workmanship), etc. Family portraits. Busts of Krylov, Pushkin and Gogol. A cabinet with stuffed birds. A bookcase. On the bookcase – cigarette holders, boxes, sticks, rifle barrels, etc. The writing desk is piled high with papers, portraits, statuettes and firearms. It is morning.

Enter SOFYA *and* KATYA.

SOFYA. Calm down! Try and talk sense! . . .

KATYA. Something's happened, milady! The doors and windows are all wide open, everything's upside down . . . The door's been torn off its hinges . . . Something's amiss, milady! It wasn't for nothing that one of our hens started crowing like a cock . . .

SOFYA. Well, what do you think's happened?

KATYA. Either Mikhail Vasilyevich has gone away altogether, or he's done some violence to himself . . . He's got a fiery nature, milady! I've known him for two years now . . .

SOFYA. No . . . Have you been down to the village?

KATYA. Yes, milady . . . He's nowhere to be found . . . Four hours I went about looking for him . . .

SOFYA (*sitting down*). What am I to do? But what am I to do? (*Pause.*)

KATYA. Let it all be, milady! After all, it's sinful! (*She weeps.*) I feel so sorry for the young master! He's taken it so much to heart! You'd never know him, the way he's looked these last two days! Can't help feeling sorry for Mr. Platonov too . . . He used to be so gay . . . Looks like death now! Let it all be, milady!

SOFYA. Let what be?

KATYA. All this love. What's the sense of it all? It's all so shameful . . .

SOFYA. Get along back to the school, Katya! Perhaps he's returned already.

KATYA. Right away . . . (*Pause.*) You really ought to go to bed . . .

SOFYA. Get along with you, Katya! Haven't you gone yet?

KATYA (*aside*). You'd think she was talking to a peasant girl! (*In a sharp, whining voice.*) And where am I to go, milady?

SOFYA. I'm so sleepy! I haven't slept all night! Don't shout so loudly! Get away from here!

KATYA. Very good, milady . . . You shouldn't fret yourself so! You'd be better to go to your room and lie down! (*She goes out.*)

SOFYA. It's terrible! He gave his word of honour yesterday to be at the hut by ten and he didn't come . . . I waited for him till dawn . . . So much for his word of honour! So much for his love! He doesn't love me!

VOINETSEV (*enters, then suddenly catches sight of* SOFYA). You . . . here? In my study?

SOFYA (*looking round*). Yes . . . I must have come in by accident . . . I didn't know where I was . . . (*She goes to the door.*)

VOINITSEV. Just one moment!

SOFYA (*stopping*). Well? (*Pause.*)

VOINITSEV. Are you leaving?

SOFYA. Yes.

VOINITSEV. Hm . . . Soon?

SOFYA. Today.

VOINITSEV. With him?

SOFYA. Yes.

VOINITSEV. I wish you every happiness! (*Pause.*) Fine stuff for happiness! The lust of the flesh and the misfortune of another! God be with you! It's your life!

SOFYA. You had something to say.

VOINITSEV (*sighing*). I'm going mad, Sophie! I'm not up to sustaining this terrible blow! (*He clutches his head; there is a pause.*) I'm standing in my study, the study where once sat my father, Major-General Voinitsev, of the suite of His Imperial Majesty, Knight of the Order of St George, a great and glorious man . . . (*Pointing to* SOFYA.) This is my ex-wife . . . (SOFYA *makes to leave.*) Wait, Sophie! (*He kneels before her.*) What are you doing, Sophie? For God's sake have pity! I'm dying, I'm going mad! Stay with me! I'll forget all, I've already forgiven all . . . I'll be your slave, I'll love you . . . He won't give you happiness! You'll only destroy yourself, and you'll destroy him too! You'll destroy Platonov, Sofya! . . . Let's bring back the past before it's too late! Platonov will agree . . . I know him . . . He doesn't love you, it's just . . . you surrendered yourself to him and so he took you . . . (*He stands up.*) You're crying?

SOFYA (*standing up*). Don't take these tears to be on your account! Perhaps Platonov would agree . . . Let him agree! (*Sharply.*) You're despicable, all of you! Where is Platonov? Where?

VOINITSEV. I gave him money. He promised to leave . . .He's left already . . .

SOFYA. You bribed him? You're lying!

VOINITSEV. I gave him a thousand roubles and he agreed to give you up . . . You're right, I am lying! It's all a lie! Don't believe what I say, for God's sake! He's alive and well, your damn Platonov! Go and take him, kiss him! . . . I still can't believe it! Is it just platonic love between you? It still hasn't got as far as the . . . serious? . . .

SOFYA. I'm his wife, his mistress, whatever you like! . . .

She makes to leave.

VOINITSEV. Sofya! You're his mistress? (*He seizes her by the hands.*)

ANNA PETROVNA *enters; she goes over to the window and looks out.*

SOFYA. Leave me alone! (*She goes out.*)

VOINITSEV (*gesturing with his hand*). Finish! (*Pause.*) What are you looking at?

ANNA. The peasants have killed Osip . . . Near the well . . . Do you see? There he is!

VOINITSEV (*looking out of the window*). Hm . . . He had it coming to him. (*Pause.*)

ANNA. Have you heard the news, my dear? They say that Platonov has disappeared somewhere and . . . Have you read the letter?

VOINITSEV. I have.

ANNA. So it's good-bye to the estate! Eh? Gone, slipped away . . . The Lord gave and the Lord took away. So much for the celebrated financial dodge! And it's all because we trusted Glagolyev . . . Promised to buy the estate and he didn't even go to the auction . . . If it weren't for him we would have gone on paying off the mortgage steadily without any nonsense . . . (*She sighs.*) It doesn't do to trust one's enemies in this life, nor at the same time, one's friends!

VOINITSEV. No, it doesn't do to trust one's friends!

ANNA. Well, my feudal lord? What are you going to do now? Where will you go? God gave it all to your forefathers, but he's taken it away from you . . . You've nothing left . . . (VOINITSEV *shrugs his shoulders.*) You've lost what you've had, but the important thing is not what you've had, but what lies before you. The whole of your life is before you, a good, hard-working life, a man's life! Don't worry . . . You're a fine lad, a philologist, you're so well-meaning, you never get mixed up in anything unpleasant, you have your convictions, you're demure, married . . . You'll go far, if you want to! The only thing is, you mustn't quarrel with your wife . . . You've hardly got married and already you're quarrelling . . . Why don't you tell me all about it? What's happening between you?

VOINITSEV. It's not happening, it's already happened.

ANNA. But what? Or perhaps it's a secret?

VOINITSEV (*sighing*). A terrible misfortune has befallen our house, maman! I don't know why I haven't told you before . . . I was ashamed . . . I don't give a hang for the estate! . . . I . . .

ANNA (*laughing*). But you scare me! Has she lost her temper, or what?

VOINITSEV (*after a pause*). She's been unfaithful to me . . . I have the honour to present myself: a cuckold!

ANNA. What fantastic nonsense is this, Sergei? You don't even know what the word means . . .

VOINITSEV. I know what it means, maman! I know in practice, not in theory!

ANNA. Don't insult your wife, you absurd creature! Oh . . .

VOINITSEV. As God's my witness! (*Pause.*)

ANNA. You're slandering her! It's impossible! Here, in Voinitsevka!

VOINITSEV. Yes, here in our damn Voinitsevka!

ANNA. Hm . . . But who, here in our damn Voinitsevka could conceive the impossible idea of placing horns on to your artistocratic head? Absolutely no one! Kiril Glagolyev perhaps? Hardly . . .

VOINITSEV. Platonov!

ANNA. What about Platonov?

VOINITSEV. It's him!

ANNA (*jumping up*). What next! Really, that's the limit! Such nonsense! It's unforgivable!

VOINITSEV. Ask her, go and ask him, if you don't believe me!

I didn't believe it, I still don't want to believe it, but she's going away today, she's leaving me! And he's going with her!

ANNA. It can't be, Sergei! It's the fruit of your boyish fancies! It simply isn't true!

VOINITSEV. The truth is that she's leaving today! The truth is that during these last two days she hasn't stopped telling me that she is his mistress! . . .

ANNA. I remember, I remember . . . Now I understand it all . . . So that's it! Hm . . . Wait, wait, let me remember it all properly . . . (*Pause.* BUGROV *enters.*)

BUGROV (*entering*). Good morning all! Turned out quite warm, hasn't it? Getting on all right?

ANNA. Yes – yes – yes . . . This is terrible . . .

BUGROV. It's raining, yet even so it's hot . . . (*He mops his brow.*) Phew . . . You get all steamed up by the time you get to wherever you're going to . . . Getting on all right, are you?

VOINITSEV (*ringing the bell hard*). Damn them . . .

BUGROV (*after a pause*). Er . . . Why I've called in to see you is that yesterday they held the sale, as you know . . . And since it's a little (*he laughs*) well it's rather a sore spot for you, that goes without saying, so I . . . please don't be offended with me! I didn't buy the estate! Abram Abramovich bought it, but only it was in my name . . .

YAKOV *enters.*

VOINITSEV (*to* YAKOV). How many times have I asked you, you good-for-nothings, you scoundrels, (*he coughs*) you villains, not to admit anyone without announcing them! You all want a good whipping, beasts! (*He throws the bell under the table.*) Get out of here! Scoundrels! (*He walks up and down;* YAKOV *shrugs his shoulders and goes out.*)

BUGROV (*coughing*). It's only in my name . . . Abram Abramovich told me to tell you that you can go on living here to your heart's content, until Christmas, if you like . . . They'll be making some little alterations here, well, but they shouldn't be getting in your way. And if there's anything at all, you can just move over into the servants' wing . . . Plenty of rooms there and it's warm . . . And then he told me to ask you, Anna Petrovna, if you wouldn't be wanting to sell the mines, in my name, that is . . .

ANNA. No . . . I'll be damned if I'll sell the mines . . .

BUGROV. Well, then, Abram Abramovich says he'll claim on his bills . . . And I'll claim on mine too . . . I've bought your bills from Petrin, you know . . .

VOINITSEV. I haven't any time to talk to you! (*He gestures with his hand.*) Do what you like! . . .

ANNA. Leave us, Timofei Gordeyevich! Excuse us, but . . . please go!

BUGROV. Very good, ma-am . . . (*He rises.*) So don't bother to worry yourselves . . . You can stay on here right up till Christmas. I'll be dropping in tomorrow or the day after. 'Bye. (*He goes off.*)

ANNA. We leave here tomorrow! Yes, now I remember . . . Platonov . . . So that's it, that's why he's running away! . . .

VOINITSEV. Let them do what they like! Let them take everything! I've lost my wife, what do I care about anything else! I've lost my wife, maman!

ANNA. Yes, you've lost your wife . . . But what did he see in that namby-pamby little nincompoop Sofya? Really, these silly men lack any sense of discrimination! They're capable of being carried away by any little bit of rubb . . . And where were you looking all the time, husband? Where were your eyes? Cry-baby! Snivelling away until she was snatched up from under your own nose! Neither of you are any good, neither you, nor Platonov . . .

VOINITSEV. It's too late, there's no point in lecturing me now! I've lost her and you've lost him . . .

ANNA. But what's to be done? Something must be done!

Platonov doesn't love her! Did you know that? He's seduced her just as you once seduced that stupid German girl of yours! I assure you that he doesn't love her! What did she say to you?

VOINITSEV. She said that she was his mistress.

ANNA. She's his fat-head, not his mistress! Hold your tongue! You kiss Platonov or squeeze his hand and he makes a great fuss of it! I'm sure they haven't done anything yet! . . . (GREKOVA *enters.*) I'm sure of that.

VOINITSEV. They have!

ANNA. You don't understand anything about it!

GREKOVA. *Here* you are! Good morning! (*She gives her hand to* ANNA.) Good morning, Sergei Pavlovich! I'm sorry, I think I've disturbed you, haven't I? (*She laughs.*) I just want to show you something Anna Petrovna . . . Excuse us, Sergei Pavlovich, we're going to exchange confidences . . . (*Taking* ANNA *aside.*) Read this . . . (*She gives her a note.*) I received it yesterday . . . Read it!

ANNA (*quickly reading the note*). Ah . . .

GREKOVA. You know, I took him to court . . . (*She rests her head on* ANNA'S *breast.*) Send for him, Anna Petrovna, I beg of you! You don't know what I've done! (*Whispering.*) I went to see the Director . . . He's to be transferred to another school . . . What have I done? (*She weeps.*) Send for him! . . . Who could have known that he'd write this letter? . . .

ANNA. Go into the library, my dear! I'll join you in a minute . . .

GREKOVA. The library? All right . . . And you will send for him, won't you? (*She hides the letter.*) Darling Anna Petrovna . . . please! I'll go, but do send for him! Don't listen, Sergei Pavlovich! Sprechen wir deutsch, Anna Petrovna! Schicken Sie, meine Liebe!

ANNA. Gut denn . . . Gehen Sie!

GREKOVA. Schon gut . . . (*She kisses her quickly.*) I'm going,

Sergei Pavlovich. You can carry on with your talk! (*She goes out.*)

ANNA. I'll go and find out everything now! You must simmer down a little! Perhaps your marriage can still be patched up. I'll go and have a talk with Sofya straight away! I'm going to get every single detail from her. You're mistaken, you're just being silly . . . You're not, though! (*She buries her face in her hands.*) No, no . . .

VOINITSEV. No! I'm not mistaken!

ANNA. Nevertheless, I'm going to talk to her. Where is she?

VOINITSEV. In her room, I suppose . . . (ANNA *goes out.*) How long will this drag on? Tomorrow, and the day after tomorrow, a week, a month, a year . . . No end to the torment! (*He picks up a revolver from the desk.*)

PLATONOV (*entering with his arm in a sling; there is a pause*). He's sitting there – crying, I think . . . Peace be with your soul, my poor friend! (*He comes up to* VOINITSEV.) For God's sake, hear me out! I haven't come to justify myself . . . It's not for you or for me to judge . . . I've come to plead not for myself, but for you . . . I come to plead as a brother. Hate me, despise me, think what you like about me, but don't kill yourself! I don't mean revolvers and the like, but . . . in general . . .

Enter ANNA.

ANNA. He's here! (*She approaches* PLATONOV *slowly.*) Platonov, is this true?

PLATONOV. It's true.

ANNA. And he dares . . . dares to speak so coolly! 'It's true' . . . You despicable man, you knew, didn't you, that this was base, despicable? . . .

PLATONOV. Now look here, can't you be a little more polite . . .

ANNA. . . . and that the wife of one friend is not the plaything of another? (*Shouting.*) You don't love her! You were just bored, that's all!

VOINITSEV. Ask him why he's come, maman.

ANNA. It's despicable to play with the lives of others! They're the same living beings as you are . . .

VOINITSEV (*jumping up*). The impertinence of him coming here! I know why you've come, but you won't amaze and dazzle us with your high-sounding rhetoric!

PLATONOV. Who is 'us'?

VOINITSEV. Now I know what they're worth, all those high-sounding phrases of yours! If you've come to redeem your guilt with rhetoric, then know that brilliant orations will not redeem one's guilt!

PLATONOV. Nor will angry shouting prove it . . .

VOINITSEV. I despise your words! There! That is how a Russian redeems his guilt! (*He points out through the window.*)

PLATONOV. What is it out there?

VOINITSEV. There, by the well, there lies one who has redeemed his guilt!

PLATONOV. Yes, I saw . . .

VOINITSEV (*sitting down*). Maman, ask him why he's come here!

ANNA. Platonov, what do you want here?

PLATONOV. Ask for yourself! Why bother maman? All is lost! My wife has left me – and all is lost, nothing is left! Sophie is as lovely as a day in May, an ideal that shuts out all other ideals . . .

VOINITSEV. I'm not listening!

PLATONOV. Voinitsev! I haven't come here to be insulted! I'm a human being, so kindly treat me as such! Unhappy you may be, but you and your unhappiness are nothing compared with the sufferings I endured after you left me! It was a fearful night, Voinitsev, after you left . . .

ANNA. That may very well be so, but who's in any way concerned with your night of torment? . . .

PLATONOV (*burying his face in his hands*). They don't understand! Who will understand? Fools, cruel, heartless . . .

VOINITSEV. I understand you! I understand the part you're playing only too well! You're a cunning scoundrel! That's what you are!

PLATONOV. I forgive you what you've said since you're a fool! But take care, don't say any more! (*To* ANNA.) And what are you hanging round for? You like violent emotions, you find them interesting? You have no business to be here! There's no need for witnesses!

ANNA. And you have no business to be here! You can . . . clear out. To have made this filthy, low, disgusting mess and then come and complain about his torments! . . .

VOINITSEV (*jumping up*). What more does he want of me? I don't understand . . .

PLATONOV. I can see very well that you don't understand! (*He goes to the door.*) I'm sorry that I spoke to you . . . I was stupid enough to take you for decent people . . . You're just the same as all the others . . . savages . . . coarse, uncouth peasants! . . . (*He goes out, slamming the door.*)

ANNA (*wringing her hands*). What a foul thing to say! . . . Go after him . . . Catch him up . . . Tell him . . . Tell him . . .

VOINITSEV. What can I say to him?

ANNA. Anything . . . Run after him, Sergei! I beg of you! He came here with good intentions and you were so cruel to him! Run quickly, my dearest!

VOINITSEV. I can't! Leave me alone!

ANNA. But he's not the only one to blame, Sergei! We're all of us to blame! Go . . . Show him that you are a human! For God's sake . . . Go on then, run . . . (*Weeping.*) Sergei!

VOINITSEV. I'm going mad . . .

ANNA. Go mad, but don't you dare insult others! Oh . . . run, for God's sake (*weeping*) Sergei!

PLATONOV (*re-entering*). Oh! (*He groans and sits down on the couch.* VOINITSEV *rises.*) My arm's aching . . . I'm as hungry as a dog . . . It's cold . . . Fever . . .I'm in pain, don't you understand? I'm finished! What more do you want of me?

VOINITSEV (*coming up to* PLATONOV). Mikhail Vasilyevich, let's forgive each other . . . I . . . You do understand my position . . . I forgive you . . . (*After a pause he goes and sits at the table.*)

PLATONOV. I'm not moving from here . . . You can set the house on fire if you like! . . . You can all leave the room if my presence bothers you . . . (*He is about to lie down.*) Give me something warm . . . to cover me . . . I'm not going home . . . It's raining. I'll lie down here . . .

ANNA (*coming up to* PLATONOV). Go along home, Mikhail Vasilyevich! I'll send along whatever you need. (*She touches him on the shoulder.*) Go on! Go along home!

PLATONOV. You can leave the room if my presence bothers you . . . Give me a drink of water! (ANNA *hands him a decanter of water; he drinks straight from it.*) I'm sick, I'm so sick, my dear!

ANNA. Go along home! (*She lays her hand on his brow.*) Forehead's hot . . . Go along home . . . I'll send for Triletski . . .

PLATONOV. I'm poorly, Your Excellency, poorly, poorly . . .

ANNA. What about me? Go home, please! Do you hear? . . .

Enter SOFYA.

SOFYA. Be good enough to take your money back! Such magnanimity! I've already told you, I think . . . (*She sees* PLATONOV.) You . . . here? Why are you here? (*Pause.*) What are you doing here?

PLATONOV. Me?

SOFYA. Yes, you!

ANNA. Come along, let's leave, Sergei! (*She goes out and after a minute tiptoes back and sits in a corner.*)

PLATONOV. It's all over, Sofya!

SOFYA. That is . . . ?

PLATONOV. Yes, that is . . . We'll talk later.

SOFYA. Mikhail Vasilyevich! What does it mean . . . all this?

PLATONOV. I don't want anything! I don't want love, or hate, just give me peace and quiet and nothing else! I beg you . . . I don't even feel like talking . . . Enough's been said . . . Please.

SOFYA. What's he saying?

PLATONOV. I'm saying that I've had enough. I don't want your new life! I don't know what to do with the old one, as it is. Don't want anything! . . .

SOFYA (*shrugging her shoulders*). I don't understand . . .

PLATONOV. You don't understand? The knot is broken, that's what!

SOFYA. You're not coming, is that it?

PLATONOV. No need to turn pale, Sofya . . . Sofya Yegorovna, I mean!

SOFYA. Cheating me, are you?

PLATONOV. I suppose so . . .

SOFYA. You're a miserable cheat then! (*She weeps.*)

PLATONOV. I know . . . I've heard it a hundred times . . . We'd be better to have a talk later and . . . without witnesses. (SOFYA *sobs.*) Better go to your room. The most superfluous thing in misfortune is tears . . . It had to happen and now it's happened . . . Nature has its laws and our life has . . . its own logic . . . What has happened is only logical . . .

Pause.

SOFYA (*sobbing*). And where do I come into all this? Where do I come in? You don't love me any more, is that it?

PLATONOV. Why all these tears? It's all so disgusting! (*He shouts.*) I'm sick!

SOFYA. I disgust you? You only needed me for two weeks? I hate you! I can't bear to look at him! Get out! (*She sobs more violently.*)

ANNA. Platonov, go home!

SOFYA (*wringing her hands*). But what am I going to do? What am I to do? I'll die! I'll never survive this vile trick! . . . not even for five minutes! I'll kill myself! (*She sits in an arm-chair in the corner of the room.*) What are you doing to me? (*She has hysterics.*)

VOINITSEV (*coming up to her*). Sophie!

ANNA. Oh, God! Calm down, Sophie! Give her some water, Sergei!

VOINITSEV. Sophie, don't . . . Stop it! (*To* PLATONOV.) What are you standing around here for, Mikhail Vasilyevich? Go, for God's sake!

SOFYA. Get away from me! All of you! I don't need your help! (*To* ANNA.) Get away from me! I hate you! I know whom to thank for all this! This won't pass for nothing!

ANNA. Tssss . . . We mustn't start quarrelling!

SOFYA. If it weren't for the depraved authority that you wielded over him, he wouldn't have destroyed me! (*Sobbing.*) Get away! (*To* VOINITSEV.) You too . . . get away!

VOINITSEV *goes and sits at the table, laying his head down on his arms.*

ANNA (*to* PLATONOV). Go away from here, I tell you! How amazingly idiotic you are today! What more do you want?

Enter NIKOLAI TRILETSKI.

NIKOLAI TRILETSKI (*in the doorway*). I'll give you such an announcing your own mother won't know you!

YAKOV. The master's orders were . . .

NIKOLAI TRILETSKI. Go and have a kiss with your master! He's just as much of a blockhead as you are! (*He enters.*) Isn't he here either? (*He falls on to the couch.*) Terrible! It's . . . It's . . . It's . . . (*He jumps up.*) O – oh! (*To* PLATONOV.) The tragedy is drawing to a close, tragedian! Yes, drawing to a close!

PLATONOV. What's the matter with you? What's happened?

NIKOLAI TRILETSKI. What's happened? And you don't even know? It doesn't even concern you?

PLATONOV. Is it Sasha? Tell me, Nikolai! As though all this weren't enough! What's the matter with her?

NIKOLAI TRILETSKI. She's poisoned herself with matches!

PLATONOV. What are you saying?

NIKOLAI TRILETSKI (*shouting*). She's poisoned herself with matches! (*He jumps up.*) Here, read! Read! (*He thrusts a note right up to his face.*) Read it, philosopher!

PLATONOV (*reading*). 'It's sinful to pray for suicides, but pray for me. I've taken my life in the midst of sickness. Misha, love Kolya and my brother as I love you. Don't abandon my father. Live according to the law. Kolya, the Lord bless you as I bless you with my maternal blessing. Forgive a sinful woman. The key to the chest of drawers is in the woollen dress.' My treasure! Sinful! Her sinful! That's the limit! (*He clutches his head.*) Poisoned herself . . . (*Pause.*) Sasha's poisoned herself . . . Where is she? Listen! I'll go to her! (*He tears his sling off.*) I'll . . . I'll resurrect her!

NIKOLAI TRILETSKI (*lying down on the couch face downwards*). Before resurrecting her you shouldn't have killed her!

PLATONOV. Killed . . . You're crazy to say that! I didn't kill her! Did . . . did I wish her death? (*He weeps.*) Poisoned herself . . . If this is a punishment, then . . . (*Shaking his fist.*) It's a cruel, immoral punishment!

NIKOLAI TRILETSKI (*jumping up*). Yes, yes, yes . . . let's weep now . . . It's so handy to have one's eyes always ready and moist! What you want is a jolly good thrashing! Put your cap on! Let's go! Oh, he's a fine husband! And they like him here: such an interesting fellow, so original! Well, come and have a look at what you've done, you interesting, original fellow, you! . . .

PLATONOV. Enough . . . enough . . . Let's do without the words . . .

NIKOLAI TRILETSKI. It's your good luck that I happened to look in at crack of dawn this morning! Well, and what would have happened if I hadn't looked in? She would have died! Do you understand that or not? Ordinarily you understand everything but the most ordinary things! Come on!

VOINITSEV. Don't shout . . . Oh . . . I'm sick and tired of them all!

NIKOLAI TRILETSKI. Come on!

PLATONOV. Wait . . . So she . . . she isn't dead, you say?

NIKOLAI TRILETSKI. Would you rather have her dead then?

PLATONOV (*shouting*). She's not dead! I can't make you out . . . She's not dead! (*He embraces* NIKOLAI TRILETSKI.) She's alive! (*He laughs.*)

ANNA. Everyone is being particularly stupid today! Triletski, what is all . . .

PLATONOV. You gave me such a scare! (*Kissing* NIKOLAI TRILETSKI.) My darling fellow (*He laughs.*) I never believed in medicine, but now I believe even in you! Anna Petrovna! Dear woman! Just a glass of cold water and I'm a happy man! I'm going mad! . . . (*He kisses* ANNA'S *hand.*) Sasha's alive! . . . Water, water! . . . My dearest! (ANNA *goes out with the empty decanter and shortly returns with it filled with water. To* TRILETSKI.) Come on, then! We're going to put her on her feet again! We're going to turn the whole of medicine upside down from Hippocrates to Triletski! We'll turn the whole thing inside out! My head's spinning . . . I'm feeling so sick . . . (*He sits down on the couch.*)

NIKOLAI TRILETSKI. He's rejoicing! I don't see what he's got to rejoice about!

ANNA. You gave me such a scare too! You should speak more clearly! Here! (*She hands the decanter to* PLATONOV.)

PLATONOV (*drinking greedily*). Thank you, kind woman! I'm a scoundrel, an extraordinarily unusual scoundrel! (*To* NIKOLAI TRILETSKI.) Come and sit here beside me! (NIKOLAI TRILETSKI *sits down.*) And you're completely worn out too . . . Thank you, my dear friend! Did she swallow much?

NIKOLAI TRILETSKI. Enough to see her into the next life.

PLATONOV. Fancy her . . . Well, thank God! My arm's aching . . . Give me some more water! I'm terribly sick myself, Nikolai! I can scarcely keep my head on my shoulders . . . If I don't watch out, it'll fall off . . . I must be getting a fever. There are little soldiers in chintz uniforms and pointed caps that keep on flashing in front of my eyes . . . Everything looks so yellow . . . green . . . You'd better give me a whacking good dose of quinine . . .

NIKOLAI TRILETSKI. A whacking good dose of something else is what you need! (*He feels* PLATONOV'S *pulse.*)

ANNA (*quietly to* NIKOLAI TRILETSKI). Take him away, Nikolai Ivanovich! I'll come and see you later and have a talk with her. Is she in danger?

NIKOLAI TRILETSKI. Impossible to say anything yet. She didn't manage to kill herself, but on the whole . . . it's a bad job!

ANNA. Go along now, Platonov, and God bless you! You need a second opinion. I'll send to the town for another doctor.

PLATONOV. There's a little upright piano crawling along on your breast, Anna Petrovna! (*He laughs.*) Go on, Nikolai, play something on it! . . . (*He laughs.*) It's funny! I'm sick, Nikolai . . . Seriously . . . I'm not joking . . . Come on then!

IVAN TRILETSKI *enters, dishevelled, in a dressing-gown.*

IVAN TRILETSKI. My Sasha! (*He weeps.*)

NIKOLAI TRILETSKI. That's all we wanted here, you and your tears! Go away! Why have you come?

IVAN TRILETSKI. She's dying! She's asking for the priest! I'm afraid, afraid . . . Oh, I'm so afraid! (*He comes up to* PLATONOV.) Misha, I beseech you, go and tell her that you love her! Drop all these wretched love-affairs! On my bended knees I beg you! She's dying! Tell her that you love her, that you consider her to be your wife! Even if it means telling a lie, please come! Do me, an old man, this favour! The Lord will repay you a hundredfold!

PLATONOV. So you've found time to have a wee nip already, have you, colonel? (*He laughs.*) We'll cure Sasha and then we'll drink together! God, how I want to drink!

NIKOLAI TRILETSKI. Father, just leave the room for a minute, will you. (*He leads his father along by the sleeve.*) Who told you that she was going to die? What put that into your head? There's no danger at all! You wait in there!

IVAN TRILETSKI (*to* ANNA). It was sinful of you, Artemis! God won't forgive you this! He's a young man, inexperienced . . .

NIKOLAI TRILETSKI (*pushing him into the next room*). Wait there! (*To* PLATONOV.) Do you want to go now?

PLATONOV. I'm awfully sick . . . I'm sick, Nikolai!

NIKOLAI TRILETSKI. I'm asking you, do you wish to go or not?

SOFYA. He should have foreseen this. I gave myself up to him without any questions . . . I knew that I was killing my husband, but I . . . stopped at nothing for his sake! (*She rises and comes up to* PLATONOV.) What have you done to me? (*She sobs.*)

NIKOLAI TRILETSKI (*clutching his head*). A public inquiry! (*He strides up and down.*)

ANNA. Calm down, Sophie! This isn't the time . . . He's sick.

SOFYA. How is it possible to hold a human life in such derision? (*She sits down beside* PLATONOV.) My whole life is lost now! Save me, Platonov! There's still time, Platonov! There's still time! (*Pause.*)

ANNA (*weeping*). Sophie . . . What do you want? You'll find time enough for that later . . . What can he say to you now? Didn't you hear? . . . Didn't you hear? . . .

SOFYA. Platonov . . . I ask you once again . . . (*She sobs.*) No?

PLATONOV *moves away from her.*

SOFYA. No? . . . All right then . . . (*Falling on her knees.*) Platonov!

ANNA. That's too much, Sophie! Don't you dare do that! Nobody is worth . . . kneeling to . . . (*She raises her and makes her sit down.*) You're . . . a woman!

SOFYA (*sobbing*). Tell him . . . Persuade him . . .

ANNA. Now you must summon up all your strength of mind . . . You must be . . . steadfast . . . You are a woman! Now, now . . . that'll do! Go to your room! (*Pause.*) Go and lie down! (*She looks questioningly at* TRILETSKI; *he shrugs his shoulders and paces up and down.*) We must take her to her room. Sergei! Nikolai Ivanovich! Well, go on, help me then!

VOINITSEV *rises, and comes up to* SOFYA.

NIKOLAI TRILETSKI. She must be given a sedative.

ANNA. I'd take some chloroform myself now . . . (*To* VOINITSEV.) Be a man, Sergei! Don't you lose your head! I don't feel any better than you, yet . . . Come along, Sophie! What a day! (*They lead* SOFYA *off.*) Courage, Sergei!

VOINITSEV. I'll try, Maman! I'll try and stand firm . . .

NIKOLAI TRILETSKI. Don't grieve, brother! We'll pull through! You're not the first and you won't be the last!

VOINITSEV. I'll try . . . Yes, I'll try . . . (*They go out.*)

PLATONOV (*left alone*). A cigarette, Nikolai, and some water! (*He looks around.*) They've gone! I must go . . . (*Pause.*) I've crushed, I've smothered these women, weak, altogether innocent women . . . One wouldn't feel so much pity if I'd killed them in some other way, under the sway of some monstrous passion, with some torture of the Spanish Inquisition, but as it is, I've just killed them . . . any old how . . . à la russe . . . (*He passes his hand in front of his eyes.*) Mouches volantes . . . Spots . . . (*He buries his face in his hands, then rises.*) I was hungry, cold, exhausted, dying . . . I came to his house, a wandering charlatan . . . They gave me warmth, they clothed me, they lavished their affection on me as on no one else . . . I've repaid them well! I'm sick (*He groans.*) I must kill myself . . . (*Approaching the table.*) Choose your weapon, it's a regular arsenal . . . (*He takes a revolver.*) Hamlet was afraid of dreams . . . I am afraid . . . of life! What will happen if I go on living? To be tortured by the shame of it all . . . (*He holds revolver against his temple.*) Finita la comedia! One intelligent swine the less! Forgive me my sins, Lord! (*Pause.*) Well? So this is death! Arm, you can go on aching as much as you like now . . . (*Pause.*) I haven't the strength! (*He puts the revolver down on the table.*) I want to live . . . (*He sits on the couch.*) I want to live . . . (GREKOVA *enters.*) Water . . . Where's Triletski? (*He sees* GREKOVA *and laughs.*) Ah! My most bitter enemy! Going to court tomorrow are we? (*Pause.*)

GREKOVA. What's the matter with you?

PLATONOV. I'm sick . . . Getting a fever . . . Oh, I approved of that . . . Very clever! Still, it would be even more clever if you didn't get tied up with me at all . . . Wanted to shoot myself . . . (*Laughing.*) Didn't succeed . . . Instinct of survival . . . Intelligence is one thing, and nature another . . . Oh, you've got sharp eyes, you've got! You're a clever girl, aren't you? (*He kisses her hand.*) Hand's cold . . . Listen . . . Will you listen to me?

GREKOVA. Yes – yes – yes! . . .

PLATONOV. Take me into your house! I'm sick, I want to drink, I'm suffering terribly, unbearably! I want to sleep and there's nowhere to lie down . . . All I want is a shed, just a corner, some water and . . . a little quinine. Please! (*He stretches out his hand to her.*)

GREKOVA. Come on then! I'll be only too pleased! . . . You can stay as long as you like . . . You don't know yet what I've done! Come on!

PLATONOV. Merci, you clever girl . . . A cigarette, a drink of water and a bed! Is it raining outside?

GREKOVA. Yes, it is.

PLATONOV. We'll have to drive in the rain . . . We're not taking each other to court, are we? Peace! (*He looks at her.*) Am I raving?

GREKOVA. Not in the least! Let's go now. My carriage is covered.

PLATONOV. Pretty thing . . . But why are you blushing? I shan't touch you. I'll just kiss your tiny, frozen hand . . . (*He kisses her hand and draws her to himself; she sits on his lap then gets up; he gets up and kisses her on the cheek.*) No ulterior motives, believe me! . . . No, I can't . . . It's all nonsense, though. Let's go, Marya Yefimovna! And as quickly as possible, please! This . . . this is the revolver I was going to shoot myself with . . . On the cheek . . . (*He kisses her on cheek.*) I'm raving, but I can still see your face . . . I love people! All of them! And I love you too . . . People have been dearer to me than anything else . . . I've never wanted to offend anyone, but I've managed to offend everyone . . . everyone . . . (*He kisses her hand.*)

GREKOVA. I understand you . . . I understand the position you're in . . . It's Sophie . . . Yes?

PLATONOV. Sophie, Zizi, Mimi, Masha . . . There are so many of you . . . I love you all . . . When I was at the university, I used to pass through Theatre Square and I used to . . . to speak kindly to the young prostitutes . . . I redeemed one, Raissa . . . With some other students I got together three hundred roubles and redeemed another one . . . Would you like to see the letters she wrote me?

GREKOVA. What's the matter?

PLATONOV. You think I've gone mad, don't you? I'm just delirious – ask Triletski . . . (*He takes her by the shoulders.*)

And everyone loves me, everyone! Sometimes you offend them . . . and still they love you! Grekova, for instance . . . I shoved her on to a table and still she loves me! Oh . . . you're Grekova . . . Sorry!

GREKOVA. Where does it hurt?

PLATONOV. Platonov hurts. After all, you do love me, don't you? Don't you? Frankly . . . I don't want anything . . . Just tell me, do you love me?

GREKOVA. Yes . . . (*She places her head on his heart.*) Yes . . .

PLATONOV (*kissing her on the head*). They all love me . . . When I recover, I'll seduce you . . . Back there it was kind words, now it's seduction . . .

GREKOVA. It's all one to me . . . I don't want anything . . . You're the only man. I don't want any other! Do what you like with me . . . You . . . You're the only man! (*She weeps.*)

PLATONOV. I can understand King Oedipus scratching his eyes out! What a low wretch I am, and how profoundly I realise it! Let go of me . . . Better not . . . I'm sick . . . (*Freeing himself.*) I'm coming now . . . Forgive me, Marya Yefimovna! I'm going mad! Where's Triletski?

SOFYA *enters, goes up to the table and rummages about on it.*

GREKOVA (*seizing* PLATONOV *by the arm.*) Tsss . . . (*Pause.*)

SOFYA *takes a revolver; she fires at* PLATONOV, *but misses.*

GREKOVA (*standing between* PLATONOV *and* SOFYA). What are you doing? (*She shouts.*) Help! Quick! Help!

SOFYA. Let me pass . . . (*She dodges past* GREKOVA *and shoots* PLATONOV *point blank in the chest.*)

PLATONOV. Wait, wait . . . How can this be? (*He falls,* ANNA, IVAN TRILETSKI, NIKOLAI TRILETSKI *and* VOINITSEV *run in.*)

ANNA (*wrenching the revolver from* SOFYA *and pushing her aside on to the couch*). Platonov! (*She bends over him.*)

VOINITSEV *buries his face in his hand and turns away to the door.*

NIKOLAI TRILETSKI (*bending down over* PLATONOV, *hastily unbuttoning his frock-coat*). Mikhail Vasilyevich! Can you hear me? (*Pause.*)

ANNA. For God's sake! Platonov! Michel . . . Michel! Quick, Triletski!

NIKOLAI TRILETSKI (*shouting*). Water!

GREKOVA (*handing him the decanter*). Save him! You will save him! (*She paces about.*)

NIKOLAI TRILETSKI *drinks the water and throws the decanter aside.*

IVAN TRILETSKI (*clutching his head*). Didn't I say that I was doomed! (*He kneels.*) Lord Almighty! Doomed! Doomed!

YAKOV, VASILI, KATYA *and the* COOK *run in.* MARKO *enters.*

MARKO. From the Justice of the Peace . . . (*Pause.*)

ANNA. Platonov!

PLATONOV *half raises himself and casts his eyes round on all present.*

ANNA. Platonov . . . It's all right . . . Drink some water!

PLATONOV (*pointing to* MARKO). Three roubles for him!

He falls back and dies.

ANNA. Courage, Sergei! It'll all pass, Nikolai Ivanovich . . . It'll all pass . . . Courage . . .

KATYA (*bowing down very low before* ANNA). I'm the one who's to blame! It was me delivered the note! It was the money that tempted me, milady! Forgive me . . .

ANNA. Take heart . . . Why are you losing your head? He's only been hurt . . . He'll be all right . . .

NIKOLAI TRILETSKI (*shouting*). He's dead!

ANNA. No, no . . .

GREKOVA *sits down at the table, looks at the note and weeps bitterly.*

IVAN TRILETSKI. Grant him eternal rest . . . Doomed . . . Doomed . . .

NIKOLAI TRILETSKI. Life is only a copeck! Farewell, Misha! You've lost your copeck! What are you all staring at? He shot himself! The party's broken up! (*He weeps.*) Who am I going to drink with now at your funeral wake? Fools! Weren't capable of looking after their Platonov! (*He gets up.*) Father, go and tell Sasha she can die now! (*He goes up to* VOINITSEV, *swaying.*) And what's up with you? Eh? (*He embraces him.*) He's dead, our Platoshka! (*He sobs.*)

VOINITSEV. What are we to do, Nikolai?

NIKOLAI TRILETSKI. Bury the dead and mend the living!

ANNA (*slowly rising and going to* SOFYA). Calm down, Sophie! (*She sobs.*) What have you done? But . . . But . . . Calm down! (*To* NIKOLAI TRILETSKI.) Don't say anything to your sister, Nikolai Ivanovich. I'll tell her myself! (*She goes to* PLATONOV *and kneels before him.*) Platonov! My own dear life! . . . I can't believe it! Why, you're not dead, are you? (*She takes his hand.*) My own dear life!

NIKOLAI TRILETSKI. To work, Sergei! Let's help your wife and then . . .

VOINITSEV. Yes, yes . . . (*He goes to* SOFYA.)

IVAN TRILETSKI. The Lord has forsaken us . . . It's for my sins . . . my sins . . . Why did you sin, you old buffoon? You went about killing God's own creatures, drinking, swearing, judging others . . . and the Lord lost patience and smote you down.

Curtain